Ben W...

Jel...

methuen | drama

LONDON · NEW YORK · OXFORD · NEW DELHI · SYDNEY

METHUEN DRAMA
Bloomsbury Publishing Plc
50 Bedford Square, London, WC1B 3DP, UK
1385 Broadway, New York, NY 10018, USA

BLOOMSBURY, METHUEN DRAMA and the Methuen Drama logo are
trademarks of Bloomsbury Publishing Plc

First published in Great Britain 2018

Cover design by StudioDoug

Photography by Samuel Taylor

A catalogue record for this book is available from the British Library.

A catalog record for this book is available from the Library of Congress.

ISBN: PB: 978-1-3500-9199-3
ePDF: 978-1-3500-9200-6
eBook: 978-1-3500-9201-3

Series: Modern Plays

Typeset by Mark Heslington Ltd, Scarborough, North Yorkshire
Printed and bound in Great Britain

To find out more about our authors and books visit
www.bloomsbury.com and sign up for our *newsletters*.

Bush Theatre

Mark Cartwright, in association with the Bush Theatre

JELLYFISH

by Ben Weatherill

27 June–21 July 2018
Bush Theatre, London

This production of *Jellyfish* is supported by Arts Council England.

Supported by
**ARTS COUNCIL
ENGLAND**

CAST

Neil	**Ian Bonar**
Kelly	**Sarah Gordy**
Agnes	**Penny Layden**
Dominic	**Nicky Priest**

CREATIVE TEAM

Playwright	**Ben Weatherill**
Director	**Tim Hoare**
Designer	**Amy Jane Cook**
Lighting Designer	**Jamie Platt**
Sound Designer	**Ella Wahlström**
Acting Coach to Sarah Gordy	**Jane Gordy**
Casting	**Charlotte Bevan with ProFile**
Stage Manager on Book	**Zoe Elsmore**
Assistant Stage Manager	**Joy Laing**
Producer	**Mark Cartwright**
General Manager	**Celia Dugua**

CAST

Ian Bonar Neil

Ian trained at Bristol Old Vic Theatre School. Theatre includes: *Be Prepared* (Underbelly / VAULT Festival), *Arden of Faversham, The Witch of Edmonton* and *The Roaring Girl* (RSC), *The Blackest Black* (Hampstead Theatre), *Brilliant Adventures* (Manchester Royal Exchange), *City Love* (Bussey Building), *Me as a Penguin* (Arcola Theatre), *DNA* and *The Miracle* (National Theatre), *Ma Vie en Rose* (Young Vic). Television includes: *Our Loved Boy, New Blood, Black Mirror, Southcliffe, Holy Flying Circus, Going Postal.* Film includes: *Interlude in Prague, Spectre, Skyfall, Kon-Tiki, Starter for Ten, Atonement.*

Sarah Gordy Kelly

Sarah trained at her mum's kitchen table. Theatre includes: *Crocodiles* (Manchester Royal Exchange), *Once We Were Mothers* (New Vic Theatre, Newcastle-under-Lyme/Orange Tree Theatre), *Walking on Water* (Theatre Centre), *Harold Pinter Shorts* (Brighton Festival), *Seize the Day* (Hijinx Theatre). Television includes: *The Silkworm* and *The Strike Series* (BBC Two), *Upstairs Downstairs* Series One and Two and *Call the Midwife* (BBC One), *Peak Practice* (ITV). Radio includes: *The Good Samaritan* and *The Meek* (BBC Radio 3), *Resurrection* (BBC Radio 4).

Penny Layden Agnes

Penny last appeared at the Bush Theatre in *66 Books.* Theatre includes: *Macbeth, My Country: A Work in Progress, Another World: Losing Our Children to Islamic State, An Oak Tree, Everyman, Edward II, Table* and *Timon of Athens* (National Theatre), *The Tempest, Roberto Zucco* and *Measure for Measure* (RSC), *The Lorax* and *Cinderella* (Old Vic), *Bright Phoenix* (Liverpool Everyman), *Beryl* (West Yorkshire Playhouse), *Nora* (Belgrade Theatre, Coventry), *Incoming* (HighTide Festival), *Lidless* (Trafalgar Studios/HighTide Festival/Edinburgh), *Vernon God Little* and *The Art of Random Whistling* (Young Vic), *The Bacchae, Mary Barton, Electra* and *Mayhem* (Royal Exchange Theatre, Manchester), *Dancing at Lughnasa* (Birmingham Rep), *The Spanish Tragedy* (Arcola Theatre), *Romeo and Juliet, The Antipodes* and *Hamlet* (Shakespeare's

Globe); *Comfort Me with Apples* (Hampstead Theatre/tour), *Assassins* (Crucible, Sheffield), *Season's Greetings* and *Popcorn* (Liverpool Playhouse), *The Laramie Project* (Sound Theatre), *Romeo and Juliet* (Southwark Playhouse), *A Passage to India*, *The Magic Toyshop* and *Jane Eyre* (Shared Experience), *Maid Marian and Her Merry Men* (Bristol Old Vic), *What I Did in the Holidays* (CTC tour), *The Plough and the Stars*, *The Hunchback of Notre Dame*, *Dangerous Corner* and *A Midsummer Night's Dream* (New Vic Theatre, Newcastle-under-Lyme). Television includes: *My Country: A Work in Progress*, *Grantchester*, *Dark Angel*, *EastEnders*, *Call the Midwife*, *Land Girls*, *Sirens*, *South Riding*, *Doctors*, *Silent Witness*, *Poppy Shakespeare*, *Bad Mother's Handbook*, *Waterloo Road*, *No Angels*, *The Bill*, *Murphy's Law*, *Fat Friends*, *Outlaws*, *M.I.T* and *Casualty*. Film includes: *Broken*, *The Libertine*. Radio credits include: *Second Chance*, *Uganda* and *Crime and Punishment*.

Nicky Priest Dominic

Nicky is an actor and stand-up comedian from Birmingham. He graduated in Drama and Media from Newman University in 2013 and completed the Prince's Trust Course Get Started with Theatre at the Birmingham Rep in 2015. As a stand-up comic he has been mentored by Janice Connolly, aka 'Barbra Nice', and performed at the Birmingham Town Hall as part of World Inclusion Day in May 2018. Nicky made his professional acting debut in *The Seven Acts of Mercy* (RSC) in November 2016. Other theatre credits include: *The Twisted Tale of Hansel and Gretel* (Birmingham Hippodrome/ Belgrade Theatre/Forest Arts Centre, Walsall/Malvern Theatre). He has been asked by the Prince's Trust to become a young ambassador, due to the success he has had in his career as a performer via the Get Started with Theatre course.

Ben Weatherill Playwright

Ben is a writer for theatre, radio and television. His debut full-length play, *Chicken Dust*, was written while he was playwright in residence at the Curve Theatre, Leicester. *Chicken Dust* premiered at the Finborough Theatre, before transferring to the Curve. He has had work performed at the National Theatre Studio, Theatre503, Old Red Lion Theatre and Theatre Royal Haymarket. In 2016, he was thrilled to be part of Channel 4's 4Screenwriting course. Since then, he has begun to develop TV projects with independent production companies and is under commission to Channel 4. For radio, he has written an Afternoon Play for BBC Radio 4 and is on a shadow scheme for *The Archers*.

Tim Hoare Director

Tim's theatre credits as a director include: *The Ferryman* (new cast director, Gielgud Theatre), *Masterpieces* (Surprise Theatre, Royal Court Upstairs), *Romeo and Juliet* (Shakespeare's Globe/Spoleto Festival), *Love's Labour's Lost* (Madrid and tour, in association with Shakespeare's Globe), *Don Juan* (Alcala de Henares), *Fred's Diner* (Chichester Festival Theatre), *Henry V* (Trafalgar Studio 2/Rustaveli, Georgia), *Bash: Latterday Plays* (Barons Court Theatre).

As associate director, theatre includes: *The Ferryman* (Royal Court/ Gielgud Theatre/Broadway), *Taken at Midnight* (Theatre Royal Haymarket), *King Lear* (National Theatre), *This May Hurt a Bit*, *Our Country's Good*, *Pitcairn* and *Top Girls* (Out of Joint), *South Downs/ The Browning Version* and *Yes, Prime Minister* (Chichester Festival Theatre and West End), *Alice in Wonderland* (Chichester Festival Theatre).

Tim is Associate Artist at Out of Joint and was co-founder and Artistic Director of the Theatre on the Fly, a temporary theatre celebrating Chichester Festival Theatre's fiftieth anniversary.

Amy Jane Cook Designer

Amy is a designer, whose previous designs at Bush Theatre include: *66 Books*, *Where's My Seat?* and *Mudlarks*. Other theatre includes: *Not Talking* (Arcola Theatre), *Lava* (Nottingham Playhouse), *Our*

Blue Heaven (New Wolsey Theatre, Ipswich), *The Rise and Fall of Little Voice* and *St Nicholas* (Theatr Clwyd), *Insignificance* (Theatre Clwyd/Langham Place, New York), *Up 'n' Under* (UK tour), *The 8th* (Barbican), *Mydidae* (Soho Theatre/Trafalgar Studios), *66 Books* (Bush Theatre/Westminster Abbey), *Mudlarks* (Bush Theatre/HighTide Festival), *Medea* (Gate Theatre), *65 Miles*, *Once Upon a Time in Wigan* (Hull Truck), *Hamlet* (Young Vic), *The Water Engine* (Old Vic Tunnels), *Glory Dazed* (Soho Theatre), *The Mobile Phone Show* (Lyric Hammersmith), *Almost Maine* (Park Theatre), *The Separation* (Project Arts Centre, Dublin/Theatre503), *Where the Mangrove Grows* (Theatre503), *To Dream Again* (Clwyd/Polka), *The Giant Jam Sandwich* (Trafalgar Studios/Derby Live/Polka Theatre), *Thumbelina's Great Adventure* (Cambridge Arts Centre), *I (heart) Peterborough* (Pleasance Theatre tour).

Jamie Platt Lighting Designer

Jamie trained at the Royal Welsh College of Music & Drama and has been nominated for two Off West End Awards, in 2016 and 2015. In 2013 he was the winner of the Association of Lighting Designers' ETC Award.

Lighting designs include: *Yous Two* (Hampstead Theatre), *Le Grand Mort* (Trafalgar Studios), *To Dream Again* (Theatr Clwyd/Polka Theatre), *The Moor* and *Where Do Little Birds Go?* (Old Red Lion Theatre), *Checkpoint Chana*, *Quaint Honour*, *P'yongyang*, *We Know Where You Live* and *Chicken Dust* (Finborough Theatre), *Beast* and *Klippies* (Southwark Playhouse), *Vincent River* (Hope Mill Theatre), *Pattern Recognition* (Platform Theatre and world tour), *Reared*, *Screwed* and *Grey Man* (Theatre503), *The Trap* (Omnibus Theatre), *The Wonderful World of Dissocia* (Embassy Theatre), *The Act* (Yard Theatre), *Constellations* (Théâtre Municipal de Fontainebleau), *YOU* and *Mr. Incredible* (The Vaults), *House of America* (Jack Studio Theatre), *And Now: The World!* (Derby Theatre and UK tour), *Make/Believe* (V&A Museum), *Ring the Changes+* (Southbank Centre and UK tour), *Mahmud íle Yezida*, *BOY*, *Misbehaving*, *The Intruder*, *Bald Prima Donna* and *The Red Helicopter* (Arcola Theatre), *My Land's Shore* (Theatr Soar).

Associate lighting designs include: *Ink* (Duke of York's Theatre) for Neil Austin, *Depart* (UK tour), *The Grit in the Oyster* (Sadler's Wells and world tour), *The Measures Taken*, *All That Is Solid Melts into Air*

(Royal Opera House and world tour) *and Our Big Land* (New Wolsey Theatre, Ipswich, and UK tour) for Lee Curran and *Machinal* (Almeida Theatre) and *Circle Mirror Transformation* (HOME) for Jack Knowles.

Ella Wahlström Sound Designer

Ella is a London-based sound designer who trained at Rose Bruford. She was an original sound operator of Complicite's *The Encounter*, a co-sound designer of Robert Wilson and Mikhail Baryshnikov's *Letter to a Man* and the sound designer of Esa-Pekka Salonen's Cello Concerto.

Her theatre sound design credits include: *Peter Pan Goes Wrong* (Mischief Theatre, West End), *No Place for a Woman* (Theatre503) *Three Generations of Women* (Broken Leg Theatre, Greenwich Theatre), *The Life* (English Theatre, Frankfurt), *The Bunker Trilogy, The Frontier Trilogy* and *The Capone Trilogy* (Jethro Compton, Edinburgh Fringe and international touring), *Empty Vessels* (Rosemary Branch Theatre), *Sirenia* (Jethro Compton, Edinburgh Fringe), *The Ballad of Robin Hood* and *Klippies* (Southwark Playhouse), *In Lambeth* (Spellbound Productions, Southwark Playhouse), *Chicken Dust* (Finborough Theatre), *Carroll: Berserk* (Spindrift Theatre, Drayton Arms Theatre), *A Study in Scarlet* (Tacit Theatre, Southwark Playhouse), *Titus Andronicus* (Hiraeth, Arcola Theatre), *Romeo and Juliet* (Hiraeth, Upstairs at the Gatehouse/ Theatre Uncut, Young Vic), *The Revenger's Tragedy* and *Henry V* (Old Red Lion Theatre).

As associate sound designer, her credits include: *Othello* (Frantic Assembly), *JOHN* (DV8) and *The Cripple of Inishmaan* (Noël Coward Theatre).

Charlotte Bevan with ProFile Casting

Jellyfish has been cast with the use of ProFile – an online video database of d/Deaf and disabled performers, built by the National Theatre and Spotlight, for the use of casting directors and other professionals in the theatre, film and television industries to discover new d/Deaf and disabled talent, and to champion this group of artists. It is a free service both for actors and users, and is the first of its kind in the UK.

Mark Cartwright Producer

Mark works at Runaway Entertainment and also produces independently. He is currently producing *Shrek the Musical* (UK tour).

Recent credits include: *Crazy for You* (associate producer, UK tour), *Kiss Me*, *BU21*, *The Wasp* and *Four Minutes Twelve Seconds* (Trafalgar Studios), *Shrek the Musical* (UK tour 2014–16), *I'd Rather Goya Robbed Me of My Sleep than Some Other Arsehole* (Gate Theatre), *Jigsy* (Assembly Rooms, Edinburgh/Tobacco Factory, Bristol/Royal Court Theatre, Liverpool), *Fireface* (Young Vic), *The Hairy Ape* (Southwark Playhouse), *Bunny* (Soho Theatre/59E59 Theaters, New York), *Blue Surge* (Finborough Theatre), *The Boy on the Swing* (Arcola Theatre).

The producer would like to thank Kate Birch and Dominic Christian, Tristan Baker, and Rosemary Squires.

Bush Theatre

Bush Theatre

We make theatre for London. Now.

The Bush is a world-famous home for new plays and an internationally renowned champion of playwrights. We discover, nurture and produce the best new writers from the widest range of backgrounds from our home in a distinctive corner of west London.

The Bush has won over 100 awards and developed an enviable reputation for touring its acclaimed productions nationally and internationally.

We are excited by exceptional new voices, stories and perspectives – particularly those with contemporary bite which reflect the vibrancy of British culture now.

Located in the newly renovated old library on Uxbridge Road in the heart of Shepherd's Bush, the theatre houses two performance spaces, a rehearsal room and the lively Library Bar.

Supported by
ARTS COUNCIL ENGLAND

h&f
hammersmith & fulham

bushtheatre.co.uk

THANK YOU

The Bush Theatre would like to thank all its supporters whose valuable contributions have helped us to create a platform for our future and to promote the highest quality new writing, develop the next generation of creative talent and lead innovative community engagement work.

If you are interested in finding out how to be involved, please visit **bushtheatre.co.uk/support-us** or email **development@bushtheatre.co.uk** or call **020 8743 3584.**

Acknowledgements

I am indebted to many, many people who were instrumental in making this happen.

Tim Hoare is one of the most thoughtful, astute and gracious people I have ever worked with in this industry. I have been extremely privileged to work with him. A brilliant director, and now friend.

Thank you to Mark Cartwright for believing in the play and working bloody hard to make sure that it happened.

Sarah and Jane Gordy are two of the biggest loves of my lives.

Penny, Ian and Nicky have been phenomenal. All three are incredibly generous actors at the top of their game. Thank you for all that you have brought to this.

Nina Steiger read this play many moons ago when it was just a germ of an idea. Thank you for remembering it. Thank you for championing it. I won't forget it.

Additionally, thank you to all at the NT Studio who have assisted us in getting the play on its feet, from providing space for the initial workshop to helping us trial an earpiece.

Jellyfish was cast with the assistance of Charlotte Bevan and ProFile. ProFile is an online video database of d/Deaf and disabled performers, built by the National Theatre and Spotlight, for the use of casting directors and other professionals in the theatre, film and television industries to discover new d/Deaf and disabled talent, and to champion this group of artists. It's already an invaluable resource.

To the entire team at the Bush – being part of this season is an honour. Thank you for being so welcoming.

Amy, Jamie and Ella – your work is amazing.

Thanks to Celia Dugua, David Lam, Hana Keegan, Zoe Elsmore and Joy Laing for all their hard work and help throughout this process.

Kate Fleetwood and Philip McGinley were part of the original workshop process for the play at the NT Studio, and their insights were invaluable.

Thanks to Lily Williams and Chloe Beeson at Curtis Brown.

Thanks to Dom O'Hanlon, Lauren Crisp and all at Bloomsbury who have created this gorgeous book.

I owe more than several pints to Adam Hughes, Francis Grin, Stewart Pringle, Carey Fitzhugh, Charlie Weedon, Suba Das, Anna Brewer and Chris Cuming, who all read the play in various forms over the years.

Thank you to Lee Mattinson for giving me some very helpful answers to a couple of questions. Sorry we still haven't had a gin yet. Soon!

I was assisted in my research by many, many people. Thank you to all who have answered my questions, taught me about Down's Syndrome, shared their stories and allowed me to be part of the conversation. Thanks for being patient and allowing me to ask: what if? Special thanks to Hector Guinness.

Simon Atkinson and Emma Michaud are two of the reasons I am able to live in London and pay my rent whilst doing this. I genuinely couldn't do it without them. Thank you for being flexible.

Finally, thank you to my new husband – Chris Lowe. You didn't bat an eyelid when I told you the play would open three days after our wedding. I am looking forward to growing old and despicable with you.

Jellyfish

For Mum and Dad, who first introduced me to the joys of Skegness

Full fathom five thy father lies;
Of his bones are coral made;
Those are pearls that were his eyes:
Nothing of him that doth fade
But doth suffer a sea-change
Into something rich and strange.

                – The Tempest,
                William Shakespeare

Characters

Kelly, *twenty-seven. Dizzying. Never still. A sense that she has powers untapped. She has Down's Syndrome.*

Agnes, *mid-forties, weathered. Strong. Jagged. Resilient. She's been made rough.*

Neil, *early thirties, thin and gangly. A beard. Kind eyes.*

Dominic, *mid-twenties, warm, a devilish laugh and an encyclopaedic knowledge of pop music. He also has a learning disability.*

Setting

Skegness: *the beach, mostly. Sand. Sea. The smell of grease and salt.*

Present day. **Kelly** *and* **Agnes** *have walked the same walk along the beach every day for fifteen years.*

Note

. . . indicates a pause or a beat.

Act One

March

The beach.

It's a nice day. Not warm by any means, but one of those spring days that takes you by surprise.

The sea is calm.

Kelly *is holding up a huge crab.* **Agnes** *is repulsed.*

Agnes   Put it down.

. . .

I said put it down. For Christ's sakes, Kel. It's disgusting. Put it down. Put it down.

Kelly *continues to behold it.*

Agnes   It ain't like you never saw a crab before is it? Looking at it like it's sommat – I dunno. It's gross, Kel. Leave it be, will ya?

. . .

We need to get going soon, I've got tea on.

Kelly   What we having?

Agnes   Oh so you can hear me.

Kelly   Yes.

Agnes   We're having gammon.

Kelly   Gammon?

Agnes   Yes.

Kelly   Like a robot. Gam-mon. Hel-lo. I am Gam-mon. I am at your ser-vice.

She makes whistles and buzzes like a robot.

Agnes   With chips.

Kelly   Surprise.

Agnes   Don't be so bloody rude. We always have gammon when we're celebrating. And we're celebrating so. You'll eat ya gammon and enjoy it. And say thank you.

Kelly   Why are we celebrating?

Agnes   I think a promotion is plenty of reason to celebrate.

Kelly *is still playing with the crab.*

Kelly   Being allowed to answer the phone isn't a promotion.

Agnes   I thought you liked it at the office?

Kelly   It's not a real office. It's a charity.

Agnes   Well. Yes. Maybe it is. But. Don't do that. Oh my God that's gross, Kelly.

Kelly   What do you think it's called?

Agnes   It's a kind of crab.

Kelly   What kind?

Agnes   I'm not sure.

Kelly   We should know.

Agnes   How?

Kelly   There's books. Or on a computer.

Agnes   Kelly, I barely remember to put a bra on most days, never mind what kind of dead crab I'm trying not to stand on.

Kelly   Well we should. Names are important.

Agnes   Take a picture of it.

Kelly   Can I use your phone? The camera's better.

Agnes *hands* **Kelly** *her phone.*

Agnes   Yeah. We'll google it when we get in.

Kelly *puts the crab on the floor and takes a photo of it. She checks the photograph.*

Agnes   Got it?

Kelly   The first one was blurry.

Agnes   Try again.

Kelly *takes another photo.*

Agnes   Better?

Kelly   Wanna see?

She shows **Agnes**.

Agnes   Great.

Kelly   You can see its eyes.

Agnes   Turn it off.

Kelly   I've made it your screensaver.

Agnes   Ohh – don't do that – change it back.

Kelly   No.

Agnes   Bloody hell. How do I change it?

Kelly   Not telling you.

Agnes   Oh my God it's creeping me out. Change it back!

Kelly *laughs.*

Kelly   You're such a baby.

She takes the phone off her and begins to change the photo.

Agnes   We need to head back in ten minutes or so.

Kelly   Okay.

Agnes   Kayaks are out.

. . .

Agnes   Early this year.

Kelly Maybe.

Agnes No they definitely are. Not usually this warm.

Kelly I'm always cold.

Agnes Well you're bizarre that way.

Kelly Even in the summer.

Agnes I know, sweetheart.

Kelly Even when we went to Spain and we went to the water park.

Agnes God knows how you didn't get sunstroke. Refusing to take that bloody cardigan off.

Kelly I don't want skin cancer.

Agnes No.

Kelly Or an old person's face like yours.

Agnes Wow. Thanks, love.

Kelly I liked that cardigan.

Agnes It fitted well.

Kelly I left it on the bus.

Agnes I remember.

Kelly I can't believe I cried so much.

Agnes You were younger.

Kelly And when we went back to the market they didn't have any more.

Agnes I've got photos of you in it somewhere.

Kelly Really?

Agnes Yeah, I'll have a look.

Kelly What should I wear on Monday?

Agnes   I dunno. What you usually wear. We could have a look for something tomorrow if you like? If you want something new? Go into town.

Kelly   Will I need a suit?

Agnes   I think you'll need to look your best. Can't have you turning up scruffy. But you've got to be comfy, too. They won't expect you to look. They know you. You won't need to wear a suit.

Kelly   I'm nervous.

Agnes   You'll be fine.

Kelly   What if people are jealous and don't like me anymore?

Agnes   They will.

Kelly   How do you know?

Agnes   Because I like you. And I'm hard to get on with.

Kelly   My tummy hurts.

Agnes   It's just butterflies.

Kelly   No it's not.

Agnes   What?

Kelly   You can't have butterflies in your stomach, Mum.

Agnes   It's a saying. An expression.

Kelly   I wonder who invented it. I've got butterflies in my stomach. Imagine being the first person to say that. Or bake a cake. Or milk a cow. Pulling on a cow's tits. That's odd, I think.

Agnes   Shall we get going?

Kelly   Sure. Can we walk back the other way?

Agnes   We always go this way . . . but it's up to you.

Kelly   Well which way do you want to go?

Agnes   I don't mind. Do you want to walk back the other way?

Kelly   I don't know.

Agnes   Because I don't mind.

Kelly *shrugs.*

Agnes   Well make a decision, decide.

Kelly   We can just go the normal way.

Agnes   Okay.

Kelly   Cool.

Agnes   Are you sure?

Kelly   Yes.

Agnes   Because I wanna do what you wanna do.

Kelly   I know.

She starts to mess with the crab again.

Kelly   I like this walk.

Agnes   Me too, love.

Kelly   I'd be sad if we could never do this walk again.

Agnes   What's that supposed to mean?

Kelly   I. Just. If something were to happen.

Agnes   Like what?

Kelly   Something bad.

Agnes   Don't be silly.

The crab pinches **Kelly**. *She drops it and screams.*

Kelly   OH GOD! FUCK!

Agnes   Don't swear!

Kelly   It pinched me! Fucking crabby dickhead.

Agnes   Watch your language.

Kelly   It bit me! Oh my God! Ouch! Oh my God – it kills.

Agnes   You're so dramatic.

Kelly   I'm serious, it's alive!

Agnes   No it's not.

Kelly   It is, it is! It's alive. Honest. I promise!

She goes to touch the crab, provoke it.

Agnes   Leave it be. I mean it.

Kelly   We gotta put it back. It might die.

Agnes   Better than a bleeding finger. Come on, Kel.

Kelly *picks the crab up gently.*

Kelly   Ssh ssh sssh sshh. That's it. Come on.

She puts it back into the water.

She turns, smiles at her mum.

Kelly   There.

Agnes   Done?

Kelly   Yup.

Agnes   Put your shoes back on then. We've got to get moving.

Kelly   Make like a tree. And leave.

She starts to put her shoes back on.

Agnes   Yes.

Kelly   Make like a baby. And head out.

Agnes *looks at her.*

Kelly   We're off like a raw prawn in the sun.

Agnes   Concentrate.

Kelly   Don't rush me.

Agnes   I'm not.

. . .

Do you need help?

Kelly   No.

Agnes   Sure?

Kelly   I'm twenty-seven years old. I can put my shoes on.

Agnes   Let me help.

Kelly   I've got hands haven't I?

Agnes   Come here.

Kelly   Let me do it.

Agnes   Let me help you.

Kelly *lashes out at her, strikes her mum round the face.*

. . .

Agnes   Kelly.

Kelly   I said I can do it.

. . .

I can do it on my own.

Agnes   I know.

. . .

. . .

. . .

Kelly   Did I hurt you?

Agnes   I'm fine.

Kelly   Are you sure?

. . .

She finishes putting her shoes back on.

Agnes   Right. Home it is, tea, and then we'll google what that crab were called.

Kelly   Okay.

She seems glum.

Agnes   You know you've always gone on about the names of things. You probably won't remember, but one of the first times I took you beachcombing, we found a mermaid's purse. You were so chuffed. Waving the slimy thing about. Laughing. I kept telling ya it was for shark's eggs, but you said you were going to use it as your purse seeing as the mermaid had lost hers. Kept all your coppers in it for the machines. Stank in the end.

Kelly   Can we go the other way actually?

Agnes   Yeah. Yeah. Course.

April

The seafront. Early evening.

Neil and **Kelly** *have got fish and chips on their laps, wrapped in paper. We can smell the vinegar and it's bloody delicious.*

Kelly   You should've brought your coat.

Neil   It's not so bad.

Kelly   It's freezing.

Neil   I'm not cold.

Kelly   Yes you are. I can see your nipples through your t-shirt.

Neil   No you can't!

Kelly   Yes I can.

He looks at his t-shirt, presses it to his skin.

Neil   See?

Kelly   They could cut glass.

Neil   Thanks.

Kelly   You'd earn lots of money if they could.

Neil   I don't think it'd be a terribly practical skill.

Kelly   They might bleed.

Neil   Don't be gross.

Kelly   They're tiny anyway.

Neil   Can we stop talking about my nipples please?

Kelly   Put them away then.

Neil   You shouldn't be looking anyway.

Kelly   They're pretty hard to ignore.

Neil   Eat ya chips.

Kelly   They're too hot.

Neil   Open them up.

Kelly   They smell so good.

Neil   You want any curry sauce?

Kelly   It makes my eyes water and my nose run.

Neil   Attractive.

Kelly   Spicy food is horrible.

Neil   You're just gonna eat them plain?

Kelly   Yeah.

Neil   No salt, no vinegar, no nothing?

Kelly   Chips are good on their own.

Neil   Dry chips. You warm enough?

Kelly   Yeah.

Neil   My arse is wet. I sat in a wet patch.

Kelly   Move up then.

He shifts up, closer to her.

Kelly   Better?

Neil   Yeah.

Kelly   We could've sat on the beach.

Neil   Up here is good.

Kelly   Let's get an ice cream after this.

Neil   Bit cold for ice cream isn't it?

Kelly   No.

Neil   If you want then. But I swear that oakey man sells drugs.

Kelly   Don't the police stop him?

Neil   You'd think.

Kelly   Well I'm going to buy us an ice cream anyway. And doughnuts.

Neil   Are you trying to give me diabetes?

Kelly   I think my uncle had that.

Neil   Yeah?

Kelly   They cut off his leg.

Neil   Oh dear.

Kelly   And then his other one.

Neil   Oh.

Kelly   He was always purple. And he had a thousand pounds in a pizza box at the back of his wardrobe. We found it when he died.

Neil   That's a lot of money.

Kelly   We went on holiday. On a plane.

Neil   Where to?

Kelly   Spain.

Neil   Whereabouts?

Kelly   Can't remember, it was ages ago. Like five years. I love airports. I had to take my shoes off because I kept bleeping. Like Iron Man.

Neil   Iron Man is the worst.

Kelly   What? I like him!

Neil   Tony Stark is the true villain of the Marvel Comics universe.

Kelly   Oh really?

Neil   Yes! He's not even a proper superhero! It's commonly accepted that he's often flat-out been the bad guy. There's loads of really interesting blogs on the matter. I'll send you a link. Then you can see why he's a reckless idiot.

Kelly   Do you ever wonder why you're still single?

Neil   Maybe you should've stayed in Spain.

Kelly   Oh no, I didn't like it there. I want to go to America.

Neil   New York?

Kelly   Florida.

Neil   Why Florida?

Kelly   The sand is white. I've never seen white sand. Sharon went at Easter and said it was awesome even though everyone had a gun and was racist. Have you ever been?

Neil No.

Kelly I'll take you.

Neil I'm sure I wouldn't be your first choice.

Kelly Well, obviously I'd rather take Eddie Redmayne. But you'll do.

. . .

Have you ever left Skegness?

Neil Of course!

Kelly Well where did you go?

Neil Lots of places.

Kelly Like?

Neil I once went to Hollywood.

Kelly In LA?!

Neil Scotland.

Kelly Oh.

Neil It's not as rubbish as it sounds. They have the Garden of Cosmic Speculation there.

Kelly What's that when it's at home?

Neil It's this massive garden inspired by the principles of modern physics.

Kelly *stands up.*

Neil Where are you going?

Kelly To throw myself off the pier.

Neil *laughs.*

Neil Don't be daft!

Kelly It sounds super dull.

Neil   Thanks.

Kelly   No! I didn't mean it like that. Tell me about it.

Neil   It doesn't matter.

Kelly   Are you sulking now?

Neil   A little.

Kelly   There'll be no ice cream.

Neil *smiles.*

Neil   My mum thought it was a shit idea too.

Kelly   I don't think it's a stupid idea. Tell me about it.

He looks at her.

Seriously, I'm listening.

. . .

Neil   It's inspired by science and maths.

Kelly   Okay . . .

Neil   So all the sculptures and stuff are designed to represent optical illusions, or black holes or the Big Bang. They play tricks with your mind. They have this amazing waterfall that flows down steps and explains the story of the universe. You can stand at the top and look down and see the whole thing unfold, or you can stand at the bottom and look up at it. You feel so small. But the garden only opens on one day a year for charity so you have to be clued up to get tickets. I begged my mum for ages to take me. I saved up for both our train fares.

Kelly   Did she like it?

Neil   Oh I went on my own in the end.

Kelly   Oh. That's sad.

Neil   No it's not. Believe me, I had loads more fun on my own.

. . .

So how's the new job treating you?

Kelly   It's good.

Neil   Told you you had nothing to worry about.

Kelly   At the minute Sharon is sick too, so I am Acting Manager.

Neil   They must trust you.

Kelly   I know this sounds mean, but I'm glad she got sick.

Neil   Yeah that sounds pretty mean.

Kelly   No, I mean. I just like being in charge of EVERYONE.

Neil   I bet you're a tyrant.

Kelly   No I'm not! Everyone just has to do what I say.

Neil   I knew it. You're a desk Nazi.

Kelly   Piss off.

Neil   Bet they're begging for Sharon to come back.

Kelly   They don't like Sharon because she has halitosis.

Neil   Nice.

Kelly   She can't help it, it's a symptom.

Neil   Of autism?

Kelly   Yeah.

Neil   I'm not sure it is, Kel.

Kelly   I was joking.

. . .

I don't know how you work all the time though. I'm knackered. I keep falling asleep on the sofa and it's only two and a half days.

Neil   Sounds brilliant.

Kelly   I'd love to work at the arcade.

Neil   It's not that great.

Kelly   I love it there.

Neil   It's different when you're there all the time.

Kelly   I'm there every day.

Neil   True.

Kelly   You should be thankful.

Neil   I'd swap with you any day.

Kelly   No you wouldn't. Not even for a second.

. . .

Neil   It's my favourite part of the day, you know.

Kelly   What?

Neil   When you come in with your friends.

Kelly   Really?

Neil   Yeah.

Kelly   Good.

. . .

Neil   Are they cool enough now?

She opens up her chips; blows on them.

Kelly   You try one first.

Neil   Me?

Kelly   Yeah.

Neil   So I can burn my mouth so you don't have to?

Kelly   Of course.

Neil   Charming.

Kelly   Go on.

Neil   Why should I?

Kelly   Because you were rude about Iron Man.

Neil   What do I get out of this?

Kelly   Depends what you want

Neil *eats one of her chips.*

Neil   I think you'll survive.

Kelly   I have a very sensitive mouth.

Neil   That seagull is gonna eat them if you don't; he keeps eyeing them up.

She holds out a chip for the seagull.

Kelly   Hello.

Neil   Don't give him direct eye contact.

Kelly   They're not so bad.

Neil   Don't feed them.

Kelly   Why not?

Neil   There's signs. They can break a man's arm you know.

Kelly   That's not true.

Neil   Do you wanna risk it?

Kelly   Do you want to kiss me?

. . .

. . .

Well? Do you?

Neil   I don't know.

Kelly   It's a simple question.

Neil   Kelly.

Kelly   What? It's okay if you don't want to; I just thought you might.

Neil   Why?

Kelly   Because I'm not stupid.

Neil   I know.

Kelly   Do you like me?

Neil   Of course I like you.

Kelly   But do you like me like me?

Neil   Yes.

Kelly   So kiss me.

Neil   I want to.

Kelly   So what's stopping you?

Neil   I don't know.

Kelly   Why?

Neil   I'm banning that word.

She turns away from him.

Kelly   You said you want to kiss me.

Neil   Yes. I do.

Kelly   Sounds clear to me.

Neil   I guess it does. Like that.

Kelly   I've never kissed someone before.

Neil   No?

Kelly   No. James King asked me to in year eleven, but I think that was a dare. Do you think I'm sexy?

Neil   I think you're lots of things.

Kelly   I have nice boobs. Look.

She shimmys her boobs. He laughs.

Kelly   What are you laughing at? My boobs?

Neil   No, no. The shimmying. It's funny.

Kelly   What does it feel like?

Neil   Kissing someone?

Kelly   Yes.

Neil   It feels different depending on who you're kissing.

Kelly   Have you kissed lots of girls before?

Neil   Girls. That's an assumption.

Kelly   Boys then?

Neil   A few.

Kelly   Girls or boys?

Neil   Girls.

Kelly   Good. Do you remember all the girls you kissed?

Neil   Yes. All four.

. . .

Kelly   Why are you looking at me like that?

Neil   Like what?

Kelly   I can't work out if you're scared of me.

Neil   You're not scary.

She kisses him.

Kelly   Was that good enough?

Neil   Not bad.

Kelly   Cheeky bugger.

. . .

The next time I kiss you, it will last a long, long time.

Neil   Go on then.

July

The beach.

It's hot.

A nice spot.

Kelly *is applying sun cream to her legs and feet. She has got far too much on her hands and is spreading it round.*

Agnes *approaches with two ice creams.*

Agnes   They didn't have mint choc chip so I got one chocolate and one strawberry and got half way back and remembered you hate strawberry so you can have the chocolate and I'll just have this, okay?

Kelly   Okay.

Agnes   I had to re-mortgage the house like to get them but. Ice cream!

She goes to hand **Kelly** *the ice cream, notices the sun cream.*

Agnes   You've got that everywhere.

She hands both of the ice creams to **Kelly**. **Kelly** *starts to lick the chocolate one.*

Agnes *rubs the cream into* **Kelly**'s *legs and feet vigorously.*

Agnes   You only need a little bit. It's factor fifty. You don't need much at all. Not really. Okay?

. . .

Agnes   New ice cream bloke. This one's got teeth.

She puts her teeth behind her lips so it looks like she's just got gums.

Agnes   Would you like chocolate sauce on that, love?

Kelly   I bet this new one sells drugs.

Agnes   Did the old one sell drugs?

Kelly   All oakey men sell drugs.

Agnes   Who told you that?

Kelly   Don't remember.

She smiles.

Agnes   He's nice actually. Although a bit leery.

Kelly   A bit what?

Agnes   Nothing.

Kelly   You're hurting me.

Agnes   No I'm not.

Kelly   Ouch. Ouch ouch ouch.

Agnes   Alright. Alright. Next time rub it in properly yourself and I won't have to do this will I?

. . .

Just moved here from Yarmouth. Says he prefers Skegness. His wife works up Fantasy Island. Pushes the go button on the ferris wheel. Makes sure your bar is all the way down and that. We could go up there later, if you like?

Kelly   Nah.

Agnes   Don't fancy it?

Kelly   It's too expensive.

Agnes   There's no need for you to worry about that. My job to worry. So if you wanna go up there you let me know, alright? Yeah? Or we can go up the arcade later. The good one. I'll win ya one of those minion things out the grabber machine. There's a bit of skill to it.

Kelly   I like it here.

She's finished rubbing the sun cream in.

Agnes   There. All done.

Kelly   I look like an albino.

Agnes   Kelly, you can't say that.

Kelly   Why not?

Agnes   Because ya can't.

Kelly *sulks.*

Agnes   What's up now?

Kelly   They're smoking.

Agnes   Who?

Kelly   Them. Over there. Chain smoking like you on match day.

Agnes   I don't smoke no more.

Kelly   Yeah right.

Agnes   I quit.

Kelly   And I'm Dolly Parton.

Agnes   Shut your gob and eat ya ice cream.

Kelly   How can I eat my ice cream if my gob's shut?

Agnes   Don't be a smart arse.

Kelly *tucks into it ferociously.*

Agnes   I dunno how you can bite it like that. Gives me brain freeze.

Kelly's *phone buzzes. A text.*

Agnes   Hottest day of the year so far. Gonna get hotter too.

Kelly   Did you bring my hat?

Agnes   Yeah.

She picks up her big bag for life. She ferrets through it. **Kelly** *replies to her text whilst* **Agnes** *is looking.*

Agnes   It's in here somewhere . . . I did pack it . . .

She finds the hat.

Agnes   Here.

Kelly   Thank you.

She gets a text. She replies.

Agnes   You're popular.

Kelly *puts her phone back down.*

Kelly   Remember when we could drive right up to the edge of the sea?

Agnes   Yeah.

Kelly   I liked that.

Agnes   Things change. Places get busier. Rules and that.

Kelly   One person spoiling it for the rest of us.

Agnes   What do you mean?

Kelly   When we found that car on fire.

Agnes   I don't think that was the only reason they banned cars.

Kelly   Dogging then?

Agnes   You what?

Kelly   People's hobbies are weird, aren't they?

Agnes   Well. Yes. I suppose.

Kelly *gets a text.* **Agnes** *tries to look but* **Kelly** *flips it over so she can't see the screen. She doesn't read the message.*

Agnes   You not gonna check your message?

Kelly   No.

Agnes   Someone clearly wants to speak to you.

Kelly   The weird thing about that car was that one minute it was here and then the next minute it wasn't. The sea came and took it away.

Agnes   The tide came in.

Kelly   That's why I like it here. Things turn up and things go missing.

Agnes   Do you remember we used to go hunting for amber?

Kelly   Never found any though did we.

Agnes   Well it's rare. Special.

Kelly *bites her cone.*

Kelly   Best bit.

She sucks the melting ice cream out of the end of it.

Agnes   Don't get that down ya new top.

She tries to put a napkin down the neck of **Kelly***'s t-shirt, but* **Kelly** *bats her hand away.*

Agnes   Suit yaself. It'll stain.

Kelly *gets another text.*

Agnes   You know if I didn't know any better I would say it's a boy texting you.

Kelly   Well it is actually. A boy. His name's Neil.

Agnes   You never mentioned anyone called Neil at work.

Kelly   He's not from work.

Agnes   Oh. Where did you meet him then? Don't remember you mentioning a new friend called Neil. Alice and Claire and Liam and Darcy. But never Neil. Keeping secrets are you?

Kelly   I don't have to tell you everything.

. . .

Agnes   Is he good looking?

Kelly   Yes.

Agnes   Do you fancy him?

Kelly   Mum.

Agnes   Is he older?

Kelly   Stop asking questions.

Agnes   Oh behave, I've got my mate hat on. Do you see my mum hat? No, see. In fact, I'm not wearing a hat, which is probably making me very dehydrated, so I cannot be held responsible for prying.

Kelly   You're tapped. You're more tapped than me.

Agnes   Don't say things like that. You, Kelly Walker, are a very shrewd young woman. Now how old is he?

Kelly   Thirty-two.

Agnes   Five years older.

Kelly   Yep.

Agnes   Well I'll have to say hello to his mum sometime.

Kelly   His mum?

Agnes   Yes.

Kelly   His mum lives in Leeds.

Agnes   Well it's nice you're making even more friends. Maybe we can have Neil over. I can cook.

Kelly   On one condition.

Agnes   . . . I'm listening.

Kelly   No gammon.

Agnes   I can only cook three things. Gammon and chips, Chicken and chips and –

Kelly   Chips.

Agnes   Chilli con carne actually you rude cow. My mother said if you learn to cook three things you'll end up getting three dates and that's enough to decide whether you like a man.

Kelly   Didn't work did it.

. . .

Maybe I'll ask him over. Maybe. I said maybe!

Agnes   And his parents. They can come over too. It'll be nice. Don't know why you haven't mentioned him before. Calvin came over with his mum and it wasn't. We had a really nice time didn't we?

Kelly   He doesn't have Down's, Mum.

Agnes   Oh.

Kelly   He's really nice. He works in the arcade. The good one. Puts the prizes in the machines and stuff. He's tall. The really tall guy.

Agnes   The guy with the beard?

Kelly   Yeah.

Agnes   That's whose been texting you?

Kelly   Yes. Neil. We come down to the seafront and hang out.

Agnes   On your own?

Kelly   Well it'd be a bit weird if everyone came with us.

Agnes   And what do you do?

Kelly   We talk about loads of stuff. Even though it's none of your business. We get chips or whatever and just talk.

Agnes   He buys you food?

Kelly   Sometimes.

Agnes   Can I see your phone?

Kelly   No way.

Agnes   I just want to see these texts.

Kelly   He's just asking me how my day's going and that. I said we were at the beach.

Agnes   Give me the phone please, Kel.

Kelly   It's private.

The phone buzzes and she snatches it up.

Agnes   Is that him? Why aren't you checking it?

Kelly   Because you're being weird.

Agnes   I'm concerned.

Kelly   About what?

Agnes   You. Now show me the phone. Now, please, Kelly.

Kelly   It's mine.

Agnes   If you can't show me the phone then that suggests to me that you could be, be in a situation that could be dangerous.

Kelly   Neil isn't dangerous! He plays volleyball for God's sakes.

Agnes   What are you talking about?

Kelly   Yeah. I saw him play.

Agnes   When?

Kelly   Don't remember.

Agnes   Kelly. When?

Kelly   Last weekend.

Agnes   So when you were at Alice's last weekend. You were somewhere else? You were. You lied to me?

Kelly   It's not a big deal.

Agnes   I dropped you off at Alice's. You asked whether you could walk round the corner on your own. I trusted you.

Kelly   I didn't tell you because /

Agnes   / because you're dishonest. You didn't tell me because you knew what you were doing was wrong.

Kelly   I didn't tell you because I knew you'd be like this.

Agnes   Like what?

Kelly   Crazy! Mad. Angry.

Agnes   Crazy?!

Kelly   Yes!

Agnes   I'm not being crazy. I just don't like this, sweetheart, because it's inappropriate.

Kelly   Why?

Agnes   Because he's a stranger.

Kelly   My dad was a stranger.

Agnes   That was so different, Kelly.

Kelly   At least me and Neil love each other. You only met my dad once.

Agnes   Watch it. You do realise he's going to be in big trouble? It's wrong what he's doing.

Kelly   He was worried you'd be like this.

Agnes   He. He said I'd be like what?

Kelly   Huge. Over the top. That you'd go right up to space.

Agnes   He asked you not to tell me?

Kelly   No. I didn't say that. Don't do that.

Agnes   Do what?

Kelly   Twist all of my sentences to make it sound wrong. Make him sound . . .

Agnes   Predatory?

Kelly   I don't know what that means.

Agnes   No. No of course you don't.

Kelly   Explain it to me then. I can understand!

Agnes   The very fact that. Can't you see? It's because I have to explain what words like that mean, what they mean in real life.

Kelly   What does it mean?

Agnes   It means to exploit, to use someone in a way that's wrong.

Kelly   Because I can't look after myself or something.

Agnes   Well you can't. You have no idea how close you are to disaster all the time.

Kelly   I hate you.

Agnes   No you don't, love.

Kelly   You have no idea.

Agnes   Kelly, he could be after anything.

Kelly   Like sex you mean?

Agnes   Yes, actually.

Kelly   Well he's not. We've only kissed.

Agnes   You've kissed?!

Kelly   It's no big deal.

Agnes   I think you'll find it is!

Kelly   Stop shouting.

Agnes   He kissed you?!

Kelly   No, we kissed. I'm a consenting adult . . .

Agnes   I don't care. You should have told me immediately.

Kelly   Mum, people are looking at us.

Agnes   I don't care!

Kelly   Stop yelling.

Agnes   Don't tell me what to do.

Kelly   You look like a horrible, old woman shouting at a girl with Down's Syndrome. An ogre.

Agnes   You think I haven't gotten used to that by now? That I was worried about people rubbernecking when you walloped another kid on the head with a rock? Or slammed my hand in the car door? Don't you think I've had people staring at me, my whole life?

Kelly   They stare at me, Mum. They stare at me. Not you, me.

She begins to lick the melted ice cream off her fingers.

Agnes   No – I've got some tissues in my bag somewhere.

She begins to ferret around in the beach bag for them.

Kelly   I'm fine.

Agnes   In about twenty minutes you'll be complaining you have sticky hands. I bet you. You will. You hate having sticky hands.

She's found them. She holds them out to **Kelly**.

Agnes   Here. Here you are.

Kelly *wipes her hands on her clothes in defiance.*

Agnes   You know I'm going to report him, don't you?

Kelly   Mum.

Agnes   I feel sick.

Kelly   I'm happy.

Agnes   I need time to think.

Kelly   I love him.

Agnes   ENOUGH.

. . .

Kelly   I really love him.

Agnes   I said, enough.

July – that night

Night.

The seafront. Outside the arcade. Car park.

We can hear the crash of the sea in the distance. The sound of the arcade. The cars along the main road.

Agnes *is in her Morrisons uniform.* **Neil** *in his arcade clothes.*

Agnes   I've been waiting out here thinking about what I should say to you.

Neil   I'm sorry?

Agnes   I'm Kelly's mum.

Neil   Oh. Okay.

Agnes   That it?

Neil   What's wrong?

Agnes   I came to tell you to leave her be.

Neil   I'm not sure what you think is going on . . .

Agnes   What do you think your boss would say if I went in and told him you've been messing about with a girl who's got Down's Syndrome?

Neil   Messing about?

Agnes   She's told me everything.

Neil   What has she told you?

Agnes   She told me you kissed her.

Neil   Kelly and I just started talking, you know. Became mates.

Agnes   Then why did you kiss her?

Neil   She kissed me!

Agnes   Don't give me that.

Neil   It was, unexpected. She caught me off guard.

Agnes   Well now she thinks she loves you.

Neil   Really?

Agnes   Creep.

Neil   Excuse me?

Agnes   Leave her be. I don't like it.

Neil   I don't understand what the problem is.

Agnes   Then let me make it clear: it's weird. So back off.

Neil   Back off?

Agnes   My Kelly's nice to everyone. To a fault. People with Down's Syndrome can be like that. And it's why people like you can get them into trouble.

Neil   She's not in trouble. I'm not sure what it is you think I've done.

Agnes   You shoved your tongue down her throat. God knows what you'd have convinced her to do if I hadn't /

Neil / It wasn't like that.

Agnes You took advantage.

Neil That's not what happened.

Agnes She says you've been buying her chips. Ice cream. Going for walks.

Neil We have.

Agnes Can't you see what that is? Separating her from her mates and taking private little walks along the seafront.

Neil I didn't really think about it . . .

Agnes That's worse!

Neil We were just hanging out.

Agnes It's grooming.

Neil No. That's very different.

Agnes You don't separate a disabled girl from her friends, cast some spell over her. Kiss her. And then tell me you're just mates.

Neil I just really like spending time with her.

Agnes Well it's gotta stop. You're lucky I'm not calling the police.

Neil The police?!

Agnes Don't you see how serious this is?

Neil I was just seeing where it went. I thought we were just mates. And then we kissed, so. I don't know. This is pretty new for me, too.

Agnes I couldn't care less how you feel, mate. Kelly says you were on about taking her out tomorrow. Seal sanctuary.

Neil She likes it there.

Agnes Do you know how many times I've been to that fucking seal sanctuary?

Neil Do you want to come with us?

Agnes Okay, so you are deluded.

Neil I told her to ask your permission.

Agnes Oh that's good of you. Maybe you should've got my permission before you assaulted her.

Neil I didn't! That's not what happened. Please don't say that.

Agnes You should never have kissed her.

Neil I didn't plan it. I don't know what else to say.

Agnes I don't wanna hear it. You're gonna go there tomorrow and tell her it's done. I'll be waiting out front the whole time. I don't care what it takes. But you will end it.

Neil I don't want to upset her.

Agnes Maybe you should've thought about that. You made this mess. You can fix it.

Neil Look, I didn't know any of this would happen when we first met. She kept asking me questions. And I got to know her. We get on really well. I love spending time with her.

Agnes Just stop. Whatever it is you've dreamt up in your head. Best mates. Being her boyfriend. Whatever. I don't care. You've already fucked this up. So you're gonna take her out tomorrow. And tell her you can't see her no more.

Neil Is that really necessary? If you got to know me . . .

Agnes Am I not making myself clear?

Neil But.

Agnes She ain't like you.

Neil No, she isn't. She's dizzying.

. . .

I thought the worst thing I could do was to treat her differently.

Agnes   Well I'm her mother.

Neil   I thought she was happy.

Agnes   She's happy watching *Casualty*. She's easily pleased.

Neil   I can come over now if you want? We can all sit down together. Talk.

Agnes   You're not stepping foot in my house.

Neil   We can talk about it properly though. Not here. Not like this.

Agnes   She doesn't need you.

. . .

Neil   I really care about her.

Agnes   Good. If you care about her, you'll put an end to it.

July – the next day

The seal sanctuary.

Kelly *is dabbing at her jeans with napkins. There's a large wet patch.*

Kelly   I look like I've pissed myself.

Neil   Have you?

Kelly   He splashed me!

Neil   Sure, sure . . .

She holds a napkin under his nose.

Kelly   See! No piss.

Neil   Okay, I believe you!

Kelly   You're the worst.

. . .

Neil   Do you wanna get something to eat?

Kelly   Not hungry.

Neil   Fair enough.

Kelly   I'm tired.

Neil   But there's still so much to see.

Kelly   Neil. We've been round twice.

Neil   Are you not having fun?

Kelly   No I am. We've just seen it all.

Neil   But feeding time is at three. We can't miss that. Let's stay for that.

Kelly   Sure, okay.

. . .

Neil   You know, I think my favourite was the seal with one eye.

Kelly   Pirate.

Neil   Yeah. He was cool.

Kelly   He can't ever be released.

Neil   That's sad.

Kelly   Do you think the other seals laugh at him?

Neil   I dunno. I hope not. Can seals laugh?

Kelly   Oh yes. Especially if they hear a dirty joke.

Neil   No way!

Kelly   Yes way. They're a very smutty mammal.

Neil   Who knew?

Kelly   Just call me David Attenborough.

Neil   You know dirty jokes?

Kelly   Loads.

Neil   I had you pegged as sweet and innocent.

Kelly   What's the difference between being hungry and being horny?

Neil *laughs.*

Kelly   I'm serious!

Neil *thinks.*

Neil   I dunno. What is the difference between being hungry and being horny?

Kelly   Where you put the cucumber.

Neil *laughs.* **Kelly** *laughs too. A throaty, dirty laugh.*

Neil   That's a good one!

Kelly   Why thank you.

She looks at him.

Neil   You make me laugh.

. . .

Come on. We don't want to miss feeding time.

Kelly   If you pay a pound, you can give them a fish.

Neil   You can?

Kelly   Yeah. Just be careful they don't bite your hand off. Or splash you.

Neil   You're still going with the splashing story?

Kelly   It's the truth!

Neil   Sure.

Kelly   Stop flirting.

She takes his hand. He lets go.

. . .

Neil   Kel.

Kelly   What?

Neil   Nothing.

Kelly   Is it the people?

Neil   No.

Kelly   What then?

Neil   Not now.

Kelly   Why won't you hold my hand?

Neil   It's complicated.

Kelly   Why?

He looks at her.

Neil   Listen, Kelly.

Kelly   You're being weird. Sad.

Neil   I am.

Kelly   Why?

Neil   Because I don't think we can see each other anymore.

Kelly   Oh.

. . .

Neil   Say something.

Kelly   Do you like me?

Neil   Of course I do.

Kelly   Do you already have a girlfriend?

Neil   God no.

Kelly   Is it because I have Down's Syndrome?

. . .

You think I'm ugly.

Neil   No. No I don't. I think you're. I've never met anyone like you before.

Kelly   It's okay.

Neil   Kelly. This has nothing to do with the way you look.

Kelly   Then what's wrong with me?

Neil   I talked to your mum.

Kelly   I know.

Neil   You do?

Kelly   Yeah. And I know she followed us here.

Neil   Oh.

Kelly   She's hardly Nancy Drew.

Neil   Well, she explained things to me.

Kelly   What things?

Neil   I don't think she's very comfortable with us hanging out.

Kelly   So?

Neil   Well she sees it in a certain way. And she might not be the only person.

Kelly   How does she see it?

Neil   Well, you and I would be, different.

Kelly   Different is good.

Neil   Yes. Of course it is. But.

Kelly   But what?

Neil   It might be difficult for us two to be together. Properly.

Kelly   Like boyfriend and girlfriend?

Neil   Yeah. In a relationship.

Kelly   So it is because I have Down's Syndrome.

Neil   Yes. I suppose. But it's got nothing to do with the way you look. I think you're gorgeous. It's more. It's other things.

Kelly   I'm allowed a boyfriend, Neil. It's a free country.

Neil   I know. But maybe I'm not the right boyfriend.

Kelly   According to my mum.

Neil   Yes.

Kelly   Well that's funny.

Neil   Is it?

Kelly   She always told me I'm just like everyone else.

. . .

Neil   She cares about you. A lot.

Kelly   Was she scary?

Neil   A little bit.

Kelly   She can be. Once she didn't speak to me for eight days because I recorded over *Call the Midwife*.

Neil   Can you not joke for a second?

Kelly   Well I know what you're gonna say.

Neil   This is really hard, Kel.

Kelly   It's all my mum's fault.

Neil   It's not.

Kelly   But she made you not want to kiss me.

Neil   She's just trying to protect you.

Kelly   I don't need protecting. I'd beat you in a fight.

Neil   I don't doubt that for a second.

Kelly   You've got tiny muscles.

Neil   Has anyone every told you you're a terrible flirt?

Kelly   No. Believe it or not. This doesn't happen all the time for me, Neil.

Neil   Well, me neither.

Kelly   Do you know how long I've waited to flirt with somebody?

Neil *holds her hand.*

Kelly   Don't do that.

Neil   I'm sorry.

Kelly   I can't look at you.

Neil   Do you want to go home?

Kelly   No.

Neil   Okay.

Kelly   Do you have feelings for me?

. . .

Neil   Yes.

Kelly   So I'm not crazy.

Neil   No. I wasn't sure how I felt at first. But. Yeah. I really like you.

Kelly   Good. So now what?

Neil   Maybe we can convince your mum to still spend time together as friends.

Kelly   It's not my mum's business. It's not anyone's business.

Neil   Isn't it?

Kelly   Nope. I want a boyfriend, Neil. I want to be in love. I deserve that.

Neil   I know.

Kelly   So you can dump me if you want. I'll understand. But it can't be because of my mum. It has to be because you don't like me anymore.

She looks at him.

October

Agnes's *house. Evening.*

Agnes *is taking* **Dominic**'s *coat.* **Dominic** *is holding flowers.*

Agnes   It's so nice to meet you, Dominic. Take a seat. I'll just pop this in the cupboard. Relax. Relax.

Dominic   It's quite hard to relax in a suit.

Agnes   You look very smart. Did your mum pick it out?

Dominic   No. It was my dad's. He died in it.

. . .

I'm joking.

Agnes   Oh thank goodness. What a peculiar thing to joke about.

Dominic   My mum says I'm about as funny as James Corden.

Agnes   Well Kelly likes jokes. Tell her a joke.

Dominic   Okay.

Agnes   I won't be a minute.

She exits.

Dominic *retrieves a roll-on from his pocket and smears it under his armpits. He smells them.*

He sits. Stands. Sits. Tries to look casual.

He notices his flies are undone. Fuck! He does them up.

Agnes *re-enters.* **Dominic** *stands.*

Agnes   Kelly won't be a minute.

Dominic   You have a lovely home.

Agnes   That's very kind of you. Do you want a drink Dominic?

Dominic   No.

Agnes   We have beer, wine, some vodka, squash if you're feeling a bit boring.

Dominic   I'm fully hydrated at the moment.

Agnes   Great. That's great.

Dominic   I brought roses.

Agnes   So I can see.

Dominic   Does Kelly like roses?

Agnes   Every girl likes roses.

Dominic   No they don't.

Agnes   I'm sorry?

Dominic   Not every girl likes roses. That's a huge generalisation.

Agnes   I just meant that they like romance.

Dominic   Are you romantic?

. . .

Agnes   Kelly! You okay up there, love?!

Dominic   So . . . do you like living in Skegness?

Agnes   Never known anything else, sweetheart.

Dominic   I like the sea.

Agnes   Oh good! Kelly loves it too. You have that in common.

Dominic   Fantastic. Do you know that the world's stocks of seafood will have collapsed by 2050 at present rates of destruction by fishing?

Agnes   Maybe go back to telling jokes.

Kelly *enters in a dress.*

Agnes   Kelly!

. . .

Kelly *eyes up* **Dominic**.

. . .

Dominic *extends his hand.*

Dominic   It's a pleasure to meet you. I'm Dominic.

Agnes   Dominic has Asperger's. And he's from Scunthorpe.

Dominic   The two aren't mutually exclusive.

Agnes   No, I meant. Now that you've moved back from Birmingham. You're not that far from us.

Kelly   Mum, can I talk to you?

Agnes   Not now love. We have company.

Kelly   You said you had a friend coming over.

Agnes   I do!

Kelly   So you and Dominic are friends?

Agnes   Of course we are! Aren't we?

Dominic   Um. We've only just met.

Kelly What are you doing?

Agnes Nothing! I thought it would be nice to all get together and have dinner.

Kelly No way.

Dominic Is dinner cancelled?

Kelly Yes.

Agnes No.

Kelly I'm sorry. It's not personal.

Agnes I've spent all day preparing this meal.

Kelly Who asked you to do that?

Agnes No one, Kelly. I did it to be nice.

Dominic This is awkward.

Agnes Let's all sit down and eat together.

Kelly I hope you have a strong stomach.

Dominic I'm actually lactose intolerant.

Kelly So what is this? Blind date?

Dominic I'm not blind. Although if that's what you're into I do have a blind friend called George.

Kelly This is stupid!

Agnes Kelly. We have company.

Kelly Did you think I'd fall for it?

Agnes I know you want a boyfriend.

Kelly *laughs*.

Agnes I'm glad you're finding this so funny.

Kelly Do you know what is funny? It's okay for me to have a boyfriend only if he's disabled.

Dominic   Should I leave?

Agnes   No.

Kelly   How did she find you?

Dominic   Online.

Kelly   What? Tinder?

Agnes   There's a forum, for mothers, parents. You've seen me on it.

Kelly   So you pimped me out?

Agnes   Don't say pimped.

Kelly   Why?

Agnes   Because it's disgusting.

Kelly   I'm not doing this.

Dominic   Oh dear.

Kelly   It's nothing to do with you.

Dominic   Is it the roses?

Agnes   Kelly, I swear to God if you show me up right now.

Kelly   You're doing that without my help.

Agnes   Sit down. Eat your food. Be polite.

Kelly   Or what?

Agnes   Try it. They'll be no lifts anywhere. Not to work, nowhere.

. . .

Kelly   The roses are lovely. Thank you.

Dominic   Oh. You're very welcome.

Agnes   Excellent! Well, seeing as you two are getting on like a house on fire . . . I better check the chilli.

She exits.

Dominic   I had no idea you weren't aware of our date.

Kelly   It's not your fault.

Dominic   Are you okay?

Kelly   Not really.

Dominic   Can I help?

Kelly   Probably not.

Dominic   Is she always like that?

Kelly   Pretty much.

Dominic   I thought my mum was bad.

Kelly   Oh yeah?

Dominic   Yeah. She's convinced I'm having a nervous breakdown.

Kelly   And are you?

Dominic   I don't think so. I'm not quite sure what it would feel like. But I feel okay.

Kelly   That's good.

Dominic   My little sister is getting married.

Kelly   Who's the lucky man?

Dominic   Woman.

Kelly   Oh.

Dominic   She has asked me to do a speech which makes me incredibly sweaty. Do you sweat when you get nervous?

Kelly   Not really.

Dominic   You're lucky then. Anyway, ever since my sister told us all, my mum keeps sending me on all these dates. She thinks I'm lonely.

Kelly   Are you lonely?

Dominic   Sometimes. I'm shy. Which doesn't help. And girls usually laugh at me.

Kelly   Well they must be idiots.

Dominic   A tiny part of me knows that. The rest. Well. My mum has removed the lock from the bathroom.

Kelly   Oh my God. Really?!

Dominic   Yeah. I can't even take a shit without her listening outside the door.

Kelly *laughs*.

Dominic   It's not funny!

Kelly   I know. I know, I'm sorry.

Dominic   So I guess you're not looking for a boyfriend?

Kelly   I already have one.

Dominic   Oh. Congratulations. So why is your mum pimping you out?

Kelly   Because she hates him.

Dominic   That's unfortunate. Why?

Kelly   Because she thinks someone like Neil couldn't possibly love me without being sick in the head.

Dominic   Well that's not true.

Kelly   And she doesn't want me to be happy.

Dominic   Does he?

Kelly   What?

Dominic   Make you happy?

Kelly   Yeah.

Dominic   Then who cares quite frankly?

Kelly   You can't say anything to my mum.

Dominic   Oh. I'm a very bad liar.

Kelly   You can't. She'll lose it.

Dominic   I don't think I'd like to witness that.

Kelly   She doesn't know we're still together.

Dominic   Oh.

Kelly   Yesterday was our three-month anniversary.

Dominic   Wow. Did you do anything romantic?

Kelly   He cooked me dinner. And we had lots of sex.

Dominic   You've had sex?

Kelly   Yeah!

Dominic   What's it like?

Kelly   Awesome.

Dominic   Just as I suspected.

Kelly   Are you a virgin?

Dominic   Yes.

Kelly   I thought I would be one for ever.

Dominic   So what does it feel like?

Kelly   Dominic!

Dominic   I'm sorry if I am being too intrusive, but there is only so much information to be gleaned from pornography and humping a pillowcase.

Kelly   It hurt the first time.

Dominic   I'll keep that in mind. Be gentle.

Kelly   But it's so fun. It gets better. *So* much better.

Dominic   Noted.

Kelly   And remember. Ask if she's okay.

Dominic   So, did your boyfriend, just, ask you? Do you want to have sex?

Kelly   I asked him!

Dominic   Brave. I am ashamed to say this. But I am unfathomably jealous.

Kelly   I love everything about sex. The smell. The feel. The taste. The only thing I don't like is foreskin.

Dominic   Why not?

Kelly   It's weird!

Dominic   Not as weird as cutting part of a baby's penis off.

Kelly *laughs.*

Dominic   What do you think your mum would do if she found out?

Kelly   She'd never speak to me again.

Dominic   Really?

Kelly   Oh yeah. She's very stubborn.

Dominic   She seems . . . high maintenance.

Kelly   That's an understatement.

Dominic   If she's watching you like a hawk, how have you managed to see each other?

Kelly   When she's at work.

Dominic   You've been sneaking out?!

Kelly   You don't have to yell it.

Dominic   Sorry.

. . .

I'm happy for you. I am. But you should be honest with her about Neil.

Kelly   That's what he said, too. He's a good boyfriend.

Dominic   Good. I'm glad one of us has a sex life.

Kelly   Is there no one you like?

Dominic   Well, there is someone.

Kelly   Who is it?

Dominic   Your mum.

. . .

I'm joking.

Kelly   That's sick!

They laugh.

Dominic   Her name is Anika.

Kelly   Is she foreign?

Dominic   No.

Kelly   What is she like?

Dominic   She's beautiful and likes Pink Floyd.

Kelly   Where did you meet?

Dominic   School. She reads the same magazines as me and loves quiz shows.

Kelly   Quiz shows?

Dominic   Yes. On the television. Her favourite is *Mastermind* so I have applied to be on it.

Kelly   That's awesome.

Dominic   I know. My specialist subject will be Kylie Minogue.

Kelly   Being on the telly would impress her.

Dominic I hope so.

Agnes *re-enters*.

Agnes I hope you like your chilli hot, Dominic, because I've just tasted it and it's taking the roof of my mouth off. How are we getting on here?

Kelly Dominic is lovely.

Agnes See. I told you!

Kelly But we are just friends.

Dominic Friends is a good option.

Agnes Well it's early days.

Kelly I already have a boyfriend, Mum.

. . .

Agnes No you don't.

Kelly Dominic told me to be honest.

Dominic I merely suggested . . .

Agnes What are you talking about?

Kelly Neil and I are still seeing each other.

. . .

Agnes I hope for his sake you're not.

Kelly Why? What are you going to do?

Agnes Report him.

Kelly He's not broken the law.

Agnes You don't know what you're talking about.

Dominic Well technically he hasn't.

Agnes Did anyone ask you?

Dominic Sorry.

Agnes   Kelly. We spoke about why it was inappropriate for you to see Neil.

Kelly   I know. And what you had to say was rubbish.

Agnes   Excuse me, Dominic. Kelly, can I have a word? Upstairs.

Kelly   Not now. We have company.

Agnes   All this time. You've been seeing him?

Kelly   Yes. We've become very good at it.

Agnes   Can't you see that he's making you lie to me?

Kelly   He's not making me do anything.

Agnes   You might think that.

Kelly   Stop telling me what I think!

Agnes   I'm glad you have been honest with me. But . . .

Kelly   Well whilst we're being honest.

Agnes   Give me a second to think.

Kelly   I'm pregnant.

Dominic   Oh crikey.

Agnes   No you're not. Kel.

Kelly   I took two tests.

Agnes   Kelly. Don't lie to me.

Kelly   I'm going to have a baby. I am, Mum.

Agnes   Kelly stop this.

Kelly *doesn't move.*

Agnes   You've just made a mistake. Have you skipped your period?

Kelly   I told you. I took tests.

Agnes   They can be wrong.

Kelly   They're not.

Dominic   I should leave.

Agnes   So he's been having sex with you?

Kelly   You kind of have to have a little bit of sex to get pregnant.

Agnes   I'll kill him. I'll fucking kill him.

Kelly   I'm looking forward to seeing my belly grow and thinking, wow, there is someone living inside me.

Agnes   You can't get pregnant.

Kelly   I am!

Agnes   Don't be stupid.

Kelly *spits at* **Agnes.**

Agnes   Kelly!

Dominic   I really would prefer it if my mother came and picked me up now.

Kelly   I'm moving in with Neil.

Agnes   Did he suggest that you try for a baby? Jesus Christ.

Kelly   No. We were being careful. But now we have a happy accident. I'm going to go live with him and have my baby there.

Agnes   Kelly. No. Absolutely not.

Kelly   Tough. Neil wants me around.

Agnes   I want you around!

Kelly   You're always angry.

Agnes   Well I have a lot to be angry about!

Kelly   It's always your life that has to be the hardest!

Dominic   Maybe we should all take five minutes to calm down.

Kelly   Too late. I don't live here anymore.

Agnes   I'll book an emergency appointment. We'll go out now and get another test. You'll be reading it wrong.

Kelly   I'm not. I'm going to pack my things.

She moves to exit.

Agnes   Just wait. Come back here.

Kelly *turns.*

Kelly   I'm moving out.

Agnes   That's never gonna happen.

Kelly   I'm taking the big suitcase.

She exits.

Dominic *and* **Agnes** *are left alone. An awkward silence descends.*

Dominic   Wow. Even by my standards that did not go well.

Interval.

Act Two

October. A week later

The beach.

Neil *in his duffle coat and* **Agnes** *in her wellies and a jumper. She is holding a box.*

Agnes Y'alright.

Neil Hi.

Agnes Has she been okay?

Neil She's settling in. It's weird. The flat. It seems like; it's lived in now. Finally.

Agnes Our place is empty. I'm taking extra shifts so . . .

She hands him the box.

Agnes Here. It's stuff she forgot – more underwear, headphones and stuff – her razor and that.

Neil I could've bought her all of that. You didn't need to cart razors all the way here.

Agnes Yeah well she'll go off on one if she doesn't have the right brand, see. She'll not have thought about it at the time, but eventually she'll turn round all in a flap if she can't find it. So.

Neil Thank you.

Agnes You'll have to help with that, you know.

Neil What?

Agnes Shaving. She finds it hard. Cuts herself. Great chunks, great pieces of skin off her legs. Slices 'em right off, so you'll have to help her with that.

Neil I will. If she wants me to I will.

Agnes   See thing is she won't want you to. But you have to, all the same.

Neil   Okay.

Agnes   You think I'm being /

Neil   / No. No, not at all. I think it's good for Kelly we're finally doing this.

Agnes   She wouldn't come unless you did too. And we all need to sit down and talk.

Neil   We invited you over.

Agnes   Is she coming or what?

Neil   She's putting some parking on the car.

Agnes   She can't work machines.

Neil   It's fine.

Agnes   She calls me every day, you know. A week is the longest we've been /

Neil   / She loves talking to you on the phone.

Agnes   Do you bring her here?

Neil   I don't really like the beach much.

Agnes   Everyone likes the beach.

Neil   Well, I don't.

Agnes   But Kelly does. Fifteen years we've walked along here. For an hour or two. And now she ain't doing that no more.

Neil   Shall we go on somewhere else? We could get something to eat.

Agnes   Don't be ridiculous.

Neil   And here I was thinking we were making progress.

Agnes   A box of her crap isn't progress, Neil.

Neil   A truce then?

Agnes   You didn't leave me much choice. She would've hated me and loved you all the same. And if she hates me then . . .

Neil   I never want her to hate you.

Agnes   But I made a decision. She can go on this little holiday. Live out this fantasy. Because I know what's coming.

Neil   I'm sorry?

Agnes   I hope you know how difficult this is. Financially. Emotionally. She will become your entire life. And she will wear you down. Have tantrums. Say impossibly hurtful things. Hit you. Spit. Despite everything you do for her. You won't last two weeks.

Neil   She's never hit me.

. . .

Agnes   I'll be there to pick up the pieces when it's too much. And you can fuck off back to whatever hole you crawled out from.

Neil   All I've ever done is care for her.

Agnes   Like when you knocked her up?

Neil   That came as a shock.

Agnes   She's not bloody barren, Neil.

Neil   We were being careful.

Agnes   Has it ever occurred to you that she might've done this herself? So she could come and live with you.

Neil   Of course she didn't.

Agnes   Do you know her at all?

Neil   The condom broke once.

Agnes   Then get the morning-after pill!

Neil We did!

Agnes Clearly not quick enough!

Neil It was the day after.

Agnes Well then what happened, Neil? She's not the fucking Virgin Mary!

Neil I don't know! I've been asking myself the same question, but the point is that it's happened. And we have to deal with this. Move forward.

Agnes Fuck you've got some brass ain't ya. You think you get to stand here and tell me we have to just deal with it? Brush ourselves off and move on? You're lucky I'm not cutting your dick off and feeding it to you. Sneaking around behind my back, going along with it, encouraging her to tell lies. Deceive. Sleeping with her. Taking her virginity in my house while I'm at work. When you should've been ancient history. I mean, are you alright in the head? You don't get off that lightly. You got her pregnant you fucking . . .! You're meant to be the grown-up in this relationship.

Neil We're both grown-ups!

Agnes Jesus, take some responsibility.

Neil I'm still here aren't I?!

. . .

It should never have happened like this. But we were afraid of you. By the time we'd agreed to tell you we were . . . She was on my doorstep with a suitcase.

Kelly *has arrived.*

Kelly Mum.

Agnes Kelly.

. . .

Can I have a hug?

Kelly *hugs her.*

She goes to pull away.

Agnes   Not yet. Not ready.

They hug a little longer. Then **Agnes** *lets go.*

Agnes   I am so happy to see you.

Kelly   I saw you two talking.

Neil   We were . . .

Kelly   Arguing.

Agnes   Where have you been?

Neil   Your mum was worrying.

Kelly   The woman in front of me clearly couldn't read English.

Neil   Kel.

Agnes   Did you get a ticket?

Kelly   Yes. It's not music theory.

Agnes   You don't like machines.

Kelly   I grew up.

. . .

Neil   How long did you put on the car?

Kelly   I don't remember. Sorry.

Neil   It's alright.

Kelly   Shall I go check?

Neil   No, no, I'm sure it's long enough.

Kelly   I have this much change.

She holds out coins to him.

Kelly   Long enough?

Neil   Yes.

Agnes   I missed ya, Kel. Seems like we've not been down here in ages.

Kelly   Neil doesn't like the beach.

Agnes   He said. We could come together though?

Neil   That might be nice, Kel.

. . .

Are you warm enough?

Kelly   I'm fine.

Neil   You're shivering.

He holds her close to him. **Agnes** *watches.*

Agnes   How do people react when they see you together? Realise. If you go out.

Kelly   We do go out.

Agnes   Where?

Kelly   To the movies.

Agnes   Really broadening her horizons, Neil.

Neil   We go on dates.

Agnes   You go sit in the dark.

Kelly   We like the cinema. Neil likes superheroes.

Agnes   Does he?

Kelly   His favourite's Wolverine. You should see Neil's comics. He's got thousands!

Neil   We correct them. If they get it wrong.

Kelly   And we ignore them. If anyone is mean. Don't we?

Agnes   That must be exhausting.

Neil   What is it that makes you so uncomfortable, Agnes?

Agnes   Excuse me?

Neil   What's your problem with . . .?

Agnes   Why don't you try living my life, Neil, and then see.

Kelly   Enough. You promised.

. . .

Agnes   How was work today?

Kelly   I quit.

Agnes   Why?

Kelly   It's making me tired.

Agnes   Did you make her do that?

Neil   No.

Agnes   Do you know how hard she worked to get that job in the first place?

Kelly   I want to stay at home and look after the baby.

Agnes   Well let's not get ahead of ourselves.

Kelly   What do you mean?

Agnes   You've only just found out.

Kelly   We've already started the nursery.

Agnes   What?

Kelly   It's gonna look awesome when it's finished.

Agnes *rounds on* **Neil**.

Agnes   A frigging nursery?

Neil   We've only started clearing stuff out.

Agnes   You can't be serious, Neil.

Neil   Why?

Agnes Because we've not spoken about.

Kelly My baby?

Agnes The pregnancy.

Neil I keep saying that it would be a good idea. To talk through our options. With you.

Agnes But there's only one option here. Really.

. . .

Kelly. Love. You can't have this baby.

Kelly But it's mine.

Agnes I'm so scared though. Worried about what might happen. It's making me sick. Not like just in the stomach sick. I can feel it right in my bones.

Kelly There's nothing to worry about. I'm okay.

Agnes 'Cept there is, Kel. It's sending me mad. I was in the queue at the bank the other day. And I began to cry. Just burst into tears. I thought I weren't ever gonna stop. They called an ambulance. Said it was a panic attack.

Kelly Mum.

Agnes You have to listen to me.

Kelly No.

Neil Agnes.

Agnes I know that might sound, but /

Kelly / No, Mum.

Agnes We have to talk about this before it's too late.

Kelly What is there to talk about?

Agnes It's hard. It's hard enough bringing up a kid, Kelly. But for you. It'll be even harder.

Kelly I have Neil. And you.

Agnes   Neil isn't going to be there all the time.

Kelly   I have Stacey too.

Agnes   Yeah – once every two weeks! 'Cos we're seen to be coping.

Neil   We could get more help.

Agnes   There is no more help. This is it.

Neil   People with learning disabilities raise children all the time.

Agnes   And what if it's not healthy? What then?

Neil   Let me take you home, Kel.

Agnes   You can't run away from the question.

Neil   If there are complications then we'll deal with them.

Agnes   It's that easy is it?

Neil   Things are changing. You of all people know that. The advances in health, research. The achievements. You only have to look at your daughter.

Agnes   It might not ever learn to walk. Have heart problems. Low brain function. Arthritis. It's a scale, Neil. Are you ready for that?

Kelly   I am here.

. . .

Don't you dare talk about me like I'm not.

Neil   I'm sorry.

Agnes   I'm sorry too. But you haven't thought this through. You would have to fight to keep it, raise it yourself, even if there isn't anything. Even if everything is okay. And if the baby does /

Neil   / Then we can cross that bridge when we come to it.

Agnes   No. That's not good enough.

Kelly   It would be harder, but it's not impossible.

Agnes   I'm not making this up, Kel. We're talking about a 50/50 chance. It could be very real.

Kelly   Could be.

Agnes   The worst case scenario is /

Kelly   / Is that what I am? The worst case scenario?

. . .

Agnes   No. I didn't say that.

Kelly   Neil, I think I should talk to my mum on my own. I'll be fine.

Neil   If you're sure?

Kelly   Yeah. I'll meet you at the car.

Neil *exits.*

Agnes   Sweetheart. Let's just take a breath. Calm down.

Kelly   I'm not having an abortion.

Agnes   Even if it's best for you?

Kelly   How do you know what's best for me?

. . .

Agnes   I'm worried about you. I don't want you to do something that could wreck your life.

Kelly   What about the baby's life?

Agnes   So many things could go wrong.

Kelly   Stop this. It's cruel.

Agnes   I'm not. I'm not – I'm just. I didn't want to argue and I was trying to be. There's no easy way to talk about this, is there? But you must realise. There are so many risks. And I don't want to see you get hurt.

Kelly   Getting rid of it will hurt me. Just the same.

Agnes   Yes and it's tearing me up asking you to do this.

Kelly   You didn't get an abortion. And you were a teenager.

Agnes   I know. But it's not the same situation is it?

Kelly   Exactly. You had to do it on your own and I don't.

Agnes   And what if Neil gets bored? What if it turns out all this is too much for him and you're left on your own with a baby? I've already had a kid, Kel; I don't want to raise another one.

Kelly   Neil loves me. He'll stick around.

Agnes   It must be nice to be so certain of everything.

Kelly   Pot, kettle.

Agnes *smiles*.

Agnes   I'm trying to figure out what the least worst thing to do here is. For everyone.

Kelly   I can wash my own clothes and cook spaghetti bolognese. Open a jar of baby food. I can sterilise a bottle. I've practised. I can't wait to wake up and see my baby every day.

Agnes   They could take the baby away. Give it to a new mum.

Kelly   I know. But I'm working really hard. I'm gonna do all the classes. Take the help. Every person is different. I want us all to be a family.

Agnes   But they could still take it. Even if you do all of that. That would be awful.

Kelly   I'm stronger than you think.

Agnes   And have you thought about how much your life will change? What sacrifices you might have to make? You're very independent right now, but when the baby comes along . . .

Kelly   You're not listening. This is what I want.

Agnes   But it's not just about what you want, Kel. Your decision is going to change lots of people's lives. For ever.

Kelly   I know. For the better. Mum. I can do this. It won't be easy all the time, but you have to trust me. I can forgive you for asking me what you just did, but. You have to promise to do this with me. Please. Mum.

. . .

Agnes   You're going to have a test. And I think it would be best if we wait to see what the results are. But if they're positive. I can't make that sort of promise. I'm sorry sweetheart.

Kelly   How can you say that to my face?

Agnes   Because I love you.

November

Agnes's *garden. Night. A small party is going on inside.*

Agnes *is smoking a cigarette.*

Dominic *enters, holding a beer bottle.* **Agnes** *stubs out the cigarette when she sees him.*

Dominic   Caught you.

Agnes   I just needed some fresh air.

Dominic   Oh yeah. That air you were smoking looked real fresh.

Agnes   Don't tell anyone.

Dominic   Your secret is safe with me.

Agnes   Do you mind if I . . .?

Dominic   No.

Agnes   Good.

Dominic   Just blow in the other direction.

Agnes   Okay.

She picks the cigarette back up. Re-lights it.

Dominic *begins to text.*

Agnes   Is everyone alright in there?

He looks up from his phone.

Dominic   We ran out of beer.

Agnes   Already?

Dominic   Yes. I had to fight Carol for this. And she only has one arm so it wasn't really fair.

Agnes   I have more beer in the shed.

Dominic   Shall I fetch it?

Agnes   You won't be able to find anything in there.

Dominic   I don't mind.

Agnes   Seriously, it's a mess.

Dominic   Is it where you hide all the dead bodies?

Agnes   Oh no. They're in the walls.

Dominic   That's not very sensible. It can make the structure of the house unstable.

Agnes   Oh.

Dominic   Your best bet is to go traditional and bury it. And bury a decoy too.

Agnes   A decoy?

Dominic   Yeah. If you bury a dead animal like a cat or something a few feet above your actual body then the sniffer dogs will smell it and raise the alarm, but all the police will find is a dead cat, think it's a false positive and move on.

. . .

I've thought about this a lot.

Agnes   Clearly.

He goes back to his phone.

Agnes   Are you texting Kelly?

Dominic   No.

He texts.

. . .

. . .

Agnes   Do you think you could?

Dominic   What?

Agnes   Text her.

Dominic   And say what?

Agnes   Just ask her if she's on her way. It started at seven.

Dominic   Did she tell you she was going to come?

Agnes   It's her birthday.

. . .

He begins to write a message.

Agnes   Remind her that Neil is invited, too.

He looks up from his phone.

Dominic   Neil? I thought you weren't a fan?

Agnes   I'm not. I don't trust anyone who doesn't like the beach.

Dominic   I can't imagine liking the beach either if my brother had drowned.

. . .

You didn't know?

Agnes   Apparently not.

He is on his phone, tapping away.

Dominic   Oh. Kelly said he didn't speak for four years.

. . .

Great excuse to avoid small talk.

Agnes   Can you just? Send her a message.

He texts.

She smokes.

He hands her his phone.

Dominic   That okay?

She reads the message.

Agnes   Yeah. That's good.

Dominic   Wouldn't it be better if you called her?

Agnes   Just send the text. Please.

He sends the text.

Dominic   Gone.

Agnes   Thank you.

Dominic   I'm sure she'll be here.

Agnes   Yeah.

. . .

. . .

Dominic   It's a good party.

Agnes   That's sweet.

Dominic   It is. And I hate parties.

Agnes   Yes. Well. Everyone seems like they're having a good time.

Dominic   I think so. Although Sharon is very drunk.

Agnes   Is she? It's not even half past nine.

Dominic   That's what I said.

Agnes   Maybe I should call her dad.

Dominic   No, she's not twatted. Just loud.

Agnes   I've just had the carpet done.

Dominic   You need to relax.

Agnes   I am relaxed. I've not even mentioned the fact that no one is using the recycling bin.

He receives a text.

Agnes   Is that her?

Dominic   It's my mum.

Agnes   Checking up on you?

Dominic   She's sent me about twenty texts about *Masterchef*.

Agnes   Don't tell me who's been kicked out.

Dominic   I wouldn't know who any of them are anyway.

Agnes   It's good this year.

Dominic   Well maybe you and her can watch it together. I hate it.

His phone continues to buzz.

Oh my God!

He puts his phone back in his pocket.

I'll reply later.

Agnes   She might think you're ignoring her.

Dominic   Yeah.

. . .

Agnes   Is she picking you up tomorrow?

Dominic   Yes.

Agnes   That's nice of her. A long drive.

Dominic   It's about an hour.

Agnes   I told Kelly you'd be staying over. She knows.

Dominic   Right.

Agnes   She'll want to see you. So.

. . .

Is your mum on her own tonight?

Dominic   My dad works away now.

Agnes   So it's just you two?

Dominic   A lot of the time.

Agnes   You must be close to her then.

Dominic   I guess.

. . .

Agnes   Kelly told me they adopted you when you were a baby.

Dominic   Oh.

Agnes   I hope that's okay.

Dominic   It's not a secret.

Agnes   That's good.

Dominic   I wasn't a baby though. I was three.

Agnes   Oh. Okay.

. . .

. . .

And your parents have always been very open
with you?

Dominic   They answer questions when I ask them.

Agnes   What questions do you have?

Dominic   That's a bit private.

Agnes   Sorry. I'm prying.

Dominic   That's okay.

. . .

. . .

Agnes   But you've always known?

. . .

You can tell me it's none of my business.

. . .

Dominic   They told me that it was a decision that all the
adults made.

Agnes   Okay.

Dominic   Because my birth mother couldn't look after me.

Agnes   I see.

Dominic   So there you go.

. . .

Agnes   It must be hard sometimes.

Dominic   This is a party.

Agnes   Yes.

. . .

I'm just interested.

Dominic   Because Kelly is pregnant?

Agnes   Yes.

Dominic   Then you should be discussing this with her.

Agnes   She won't talk to me.

. . .

Dominic. I'd really appreciate being able to talk about this. If you're. You don't have to. Obviously. But.

. . .

I'll get the shed key.

Dominic   Did Kelly ask you to talk to me?

Agnes   No. But maybe you could chat to her about it?

Dominic   Why?

Agnes   Because. She might have questions. About adoption.

Dominic   You're the one who's asking all the questions.

. . .

Agnes   She might have to give the baby away. If she keeps it. And you're her friend. So. I thought. Well, it might help if you talk to her.

Dominic   Then why didn't you just come out and ask me?

. . .

Agnes   I'm sorry. I just want her to. I dunno. You've had a good life.

Dominic   How do you know that?

Agnes   I mean, you seem happy. Even though you've never met your real parents.

Dominic   I grew up with my 'real' parents. They're the ones who stuck their necks out to bring me up.

Agnes   That came out wrong.

Dominic   Do you want her to give the baby up?

Agnes   What I'm saying is she might not have a choice.
And I'd rather she be prepared. Know that things can turn
out okay.

Dominic   Things weren't always okay. I'd worry that my
mum wouldn't pick me up from school. I didn't go to a
sleepover until I was fourteen and when I did I faked an
earache so my dad would come get me. I was angry for a
long time. It's very complicated.

Agnes   That's why I'm trying to understand.

Dominic   Can you imagine not having a beginning?

. . .

That probably sounds odd. I just think part of knowing who
you are is knowing where you come from. That's all.

Agnes   I can't imagine not having. All the facts.

. . .

Dominic   You know, for ages I thought she must like
quizzes because I do. I've done every pub quiz in north
Lincolnshire. Thought she might be on a team or
something. How stupid is that?

Agnes   I don't think that's stupid.

. . .

Are you angry? With her. Your . . .

Dominic   Birth mum.

Agnes   Yes.

Dominic   Sometimes. And disappointed. And happy, that I
do have a great family. It's loads of things. At the same time.
All at once. But you kind of just try and get it to make sense.

Agnes   I really do think it would help Kelly to hear this.

Dominic No it wouldn't. Because it's not the same. My mum couldn't cope and it wasn't safe for me to live with her. And I'll never know whether or not she wishes she fought harder to keep me. I've had a hard time accepting all of that, especially with my disability. Now I feel good about myself but I didn't always. And it wouldn't make it any easier for Kelly if she heard me say any of this. Because she loves that baby already and it's not even here yet. And if she had to give it up she'd want me to tell her that it would be okay. That the baby would forgive her and be happy and have a good life and all of those things. But I don't know that. And I'm not going to lie to her. Okay?

Neil *has entered.*

Neil They said you were out here.

Agnes Neil!

Neil Everything alright?

Agnes Yeah. Yeah, we were just talking. Where is she?

. . .

Dominic I'm gonna go and call my mum. Ask her to pick me up.

Agnes Are you sure?

Dominic Yeah.

He exits.

. . .

Agnes Where's Kelly?

Neil I tried.

. . .

Agnes All of her friends are here.

Neil I know.

Agnes   What do I say to them?

. . .

Neil   I can stay. If you like? Help you clean up.

Agnes   No. You should go.

Neil   I don't mind.

Agnes   I'll cut you some cake. You can take it to her. Okay?

Neil   Sure.

Agnes   Tell her I didn't make it, so it's safe to eat.

Neil   Okay!

. . .

Agnes   Did she say why?

. . .

. . .

I'll cut you some cake.

December

Neil's *house. Afternoon.*

Kelly   You're disgusting! Gross!

Neil   No, I'm not! Everybody does it.

Kelly   I don't!

Neil   Look, I'm sorry!

Kelly   You should be.

Neil   What are you doing?

Kelly   Calling my mum.

Neil   What? Why?

Kelly   I don't want to stay here tonight.

Neil   Kel. You can't just run to your mum because we have a fight.

He goes to take the phone off of her.

Kelly   Oi!

Neil   Kel, let's talk about this.

Kelly   No. Take your dirty hands over there.

Neil   Wanking is not a crime, Kel!

Kelly   Give me the phone.

Neil   No. I don't want you talking to your mum about this.

Kelly   I can if I want to.

Neil   But it's none of her business.

Kelly   I don't want to stay here. I'm too mad at you.

Neil   We have to be able to work through these things on our own.

Kelly   You can't hold me hostage.

Neil   Stop being so dramatic.

Kelly   I thought you liked me.

Neil   Don't start. Of course I like you. That has nothing to do with whether or not I like you.

Kelly   You're meant to want to have sex with me.

Neil   I do! I do!

Kelly   Then why do that?

Neil   Because.

Kelly   Because what?

Neil   Don't make me say it.

Kelly Come on.

Neil Because I was horny, okay? Because I was horny. Jesus. It's completely normal.

Kelly What you were watching wasn't normal.

Neil It was porn!

Kelly It was disgusting. I saw the screen.

Neil They were doing it missionary!

Kelly Is that what you want? Skinny blonde girls with big tits?

Neil Well would you rather they all had learning disabilities?

Kelly I don't want you to watch it at all!

Neil It's fantasy. That's all.

Kelly Am I just a fantasy, Neil? A fetish.

Neil No, of course not! It's porn. Everyone does it. I really don't see what the big deal is.

Kelly We're supposed to be on our best behaviour at the minute.

Neil Best behaviour? Everybody wanks, Kelly.

Kelly Not at the dining-room table. Where they eat food.

Neil I'll do it in the bathroom next time.

Kelly Next time?

Neil This argument is ridiculous. You came home early!

Kelly Oh, so it's my fault?!

Neil No. I just mean, five minutes later and you wouldn't have known. It's not a big deal.

Kelly What are you doing home anyway?

. . .

Neil   I.

Kelly   I thought you finished at six?

Neil   I finished early.

Kelly   That never happens.

Neil   I didn't feel very well that's all.

Kelly   You're well enough to wank.

Neil   I just. I came home early. That's all.

Kelly   Don't lie. What's going on?

Neil   Look. Don't be mad.

Kelly   About what?

. . .

About what, Neil?

Neil   I lost my job.

. . .

Kelly   You got fired?

Neil   I quit.

. . .

I'll get a new job.

. . .

Kelly   Why did you quit?

Neil   You know the way he speaks to me.

Kelly   We need the money.

Neil   Not that badly.

Kelly   Ignore him.

Neil   I'm not being treated like that, Kelly. We get enough abuse on the street; I don't have to put up with it at work too.

Kelly   Maybe he'll take you back.

Neil   I'm not going back.

Kelly   Why not?

Neil   He thinks I'm a freak.

Kelly   How do you know that?

Neil   Because he calls me a paedophile.

Kelly   But you're not.

Neil   I am aware of that, thanks.

Kelly   You shouldn't let it bother you.

Neil   Well it does, Kel. A lot.

Kelly   Can you ask for your job back?

Neil   I'll find something else.

Kelly   Just like that?

Neil   Maybe.

Kelly   Not if everyone thinks the same.

Neil   Thanks for the positive outlook.

Kelly   Everyone knows about us.

Neil   Then I'll have to drive to Lincoln or something won't I?

Kelly   That's far.

Neil   Well I don't have a choice. This is my life now.

Kelly   And that's my fault?

Neil   No.

Kelly   Because that's what it sounded like.

Neil What is wrong with you today?!

Kelly Wrong with me?!

Neil You've been at my throat the minute you walked through the door.

Kelly Because I caught you being disgusting!

Neil Can't you give me a break?

Kelly No. You quit.

Neil I've worked there for nearly ten years. I'm going to miss it. Maybe you could try being a bit more sensitive.

Kelly Maybe you could have thought about the baby when you had a tantrum!

Neil That's not fair.

Kelly Isn't it? What are they going to say when they find out you have no job?

Neil I promise you I'll get another job.

Kelly Not good enough. They could take the baby from us.

Neil They won't.

Kelly What if they look at your internet history?

Neil Don't be stupid.

Kelly Don't call me that!

Neil I'm sorry – that was a bad choice of word.

Kelly Pig.

Neil Excuse me?

Kelly Don't you dare call me stupid.

Neil I said I was sorry!

Kelly   Yes! You keep saying! Sorry for wanking! Sorry for quitting! Sorry for calling you stupid! Sorry for being pathetic!

Neil   Oh that's right. I forgot. You're a saint.

Kelly   At least I'm trying to keep our baby.

Neil   And I'm not?

Kelly   You're fucking it up!

Neil   Well we can't all be perfect.

Kelly   It'll be your fault if they take her.

Neil   Take it back.

Kelly   Make me.

Neil   Don't shout.

Kelly   I can do what I like. It's my flat!

Neil   Well it isn't, is it?

. . .

December. The same night

Agnes's *house. Night.*

Agnes *carefully shaves* **Kelly**'s *legs. A ritual. It's gentle and intimate. Loving.*

Her daughter has come home.

January

The seafront.

Dominic *and* **Kelly** *sit on the beach in their coats. She has a set of cue cards.*

Kelly   What award did she win at the 2008 Brit Awards?

Dominic   Best International Singer.

Kelly   Correct! Who co-wrote 'Spinning Around'?

Dominic   Cathy Dennis. No, Paula Abdul!

Kelly   Correct. What Kylie song is featured on the soundtrack of the movie *Scooby-Doo*?

Dominic   'Whenever You Feel Like It'.

Kelly   Correct. Which single from *Fever* did not get a US release?

He's stumped.

Dominic   Um. Oh God. Let me think.

Kelly *starts to hum the* Countdown *music.*

Dominic   No, don't do that!

Kelly   Tick tock!

Dominic   I don't know! I don't know! Um, 'Love at First Sight'?

Kelly   Wrong! It's . . . 'In Your Eyes'.

Dominic   Of course! You know, John Humphrys would not be so distracting.

Kelly   Who knows? He might whop his dick out mid-performance. Start waving it around.

Dominic   Thanks for that image.

Kelly   I'm out of questions. You only got one wrong.

Dominic   One too many.

Kelly   You're going to smash it. I can feel it.

Dominic   I still can't believe I got on.

Kelly   Anika is going to be very impressed when you're a celebrity.

Dominic   I am not going to get famous from *Mastermind*.

Kelly   Anything is possible.

He pushes her lightly.

Dominic   Don't take the piss.

Kelly   I'm not. I'm proud of you.

Dominic   And I'm proud of you for finally leaving the house.

Kelly   I have missed the beach.

Dominic   Yes. The sweet stench of donkey shit.

Kelly   Hey! It's much nicer than Scunthorpe.

Dominic   A beach in Chernobyl would be nicer than Scunthorpe.

Kelly   Fair point.

Dominic   Do you know what the highest ever score on *Mastermind* is?

Kelly   No. No one needs to know that.

Dominic   It's forty-one points. Set by Kevin Ashman in 1995.

Kelly   What was his subject?

Dominic   The Life of Martin Luther King.

Kelly   Cool.

Dominic   I'm determined to beat it. Then she would really notice me.

Kelly   I'm sure she notices you anyway.

Dominic   Nope.

Kelly   How could she not?

He looks at her. He's unconvinced.

Kelly   Can I ask a question?

Dominic   Sure.

Kelly   What if she doesn't watch?

Dominic   Of course she'll watch.

Kelly   Okay. Well. What if she watches and is just like, oh, that's great. Well done.

Dominic   I'd be happy.

Kelly   But will you tell her how you feel?

Dominic   What if she laughs?

Kelly   Then she's not worth it.

Dominic   I'm hardly a catch. I don't drive. I hate going out for dinner because menus confuse me. My mum cuts my hair because I hate the hairdressers.

Kelly   Millions of people are going to see how smart you are. Trust me, you're a catch.

Dominic   I haven't done anything. Been anywhere.

Kelly   Excuses. You should tell her how you feel.

Dominic   She won't want me.

Kelly   How do you know?

Dominic   Because I don't see my life having great things in it.

. . .

She holds his hand.

They sit.

Dominic   What's that for?

Kelly   No reason.

Dominic   I don't like people touching me.

Kelly   Stop being a baby.

Dominic   I'm not!

Kelly   She might not be your happy ending but you deserve one. Do you hear me?

She lets go of his hand.

Dominic   Soppy cow.

Kelly   Oi!

Dominic   Thank you.

Kelly   And thank you for calling me! I've missed the beach.

Dominic   I suppose I was slightly concerned for your well-being.

Kelly   You should be!

Dominic   Is she driving you mad?

Kelly   Oh yes.

Dominic   And what about the baby?

Kelly   She doesn't mention it.

Dominic   She does realise a real human is going to eventually come out of you?

Kelly   God knows.

Dominic   I read somewhere that it's like shitting a knife.

She hits him.

Dominic   Ow!

Kelly   You deserved that.

Dominic   Maybe.

Kelly   If you're not careful I'll make you my birth partner.

. . .

Dominic Have you spoken to him yet?

Kelly No. But he won't stop calling me.

Dominic You should answer.

Kelly It's hard.

Dominic Important things are.

Kelly Who told you that?

Dominic My granddad.

Kelly Do you think he's right?

Dominic Probably. He always correctly predicted the winner of the Eurovision Song Contest.

Kelly That's awesome.

. . .

Dominic Do you think you can forgive Neil?

Kelly Can we go back to *Mastermind*?

Dominic Answer the question.

Kelly He quit his job. He should never have done it.

Dominic Was he happy?

Kelly No. But people are dickheads. Get over it.

Dominic Maybe Neil isn't used to it.

Kelly Of course he is. He's a man who plays volleyball.

Dominic People can't say stuff and get away with it.

Kelly It was selfish.

Dominic Yes. But he refused to apologise for being in love with you. That's cool. Isn't it?

. . .

Kelly Relationships are shit. Are you sure you want one?

Dominic   I think we all deserve to be as miserable as each other.

Kelly *laughs*.

Dominic   Is that the only reason you haven't talked to him?

Kelly   I guess not.

Dominic   What else is it?

Kelly   I'm worried about the test. What he'll say.

Dominic   You told me he wants to keep the baby whatever happens.

Kelly   But maybe he has to say that. Because of me.

Dominic   Well, from what I know, loving people is trusting they're telling you the truth.

. . .

When's the test?

Kelly   Two weeks. It's amazing they can tell. When you're so small.

Dominic   Wait till the new tests arrive. These ones will seem medieval.

. . .

Kelly   Do you think there will be people like us around for ever?

Dominic   People who like Skegness?

Kelly   You know what I mean.

. . .

Dominic   I don't know. If somewhere like Iceland can . . . then. I think I need easier questions this early in the morning.

Kelly   This will be easier. Tell Anika you like her.

Dominic   Call Neil.

Kelly   I will if you will.

Dominic   Deal.

He hands her the question cards.

Dominic   Test me again.

. . .

January. Two weeks later

Agnes*'s house.* **Neil** *and* **Agnes***.*

Agnes   She's asleep.

Neil   Still?

Agnes   Yeah. Maybe it's best if she stays here tonight. It took it out of her.

Neil   Okay. Sure.

. . .

Agnes   Do you want a drink or owt?

Neil   I'm trying to cut down on coffee.

Agnes   Vodka do then?

She gets vodka out and pours them both a glass.

Neil   I shouldn't.

Agnes   I'm offering you a drink in my own house. Take the small victories, Neil.

Neil   Then I'd love some.

Agnes   That's the spirit.

. . .

Neil   Your house is lovely.

Agnes   No, it's not.

She hands him a glass.

Agnes   You drink it neat, right?

Neil   Um . . .

Agnes   It's good stuff this. Not cheap.

Neil   Thanks.

. . .

The needle was bigger than I expected. I almost passed out.

Agnes   Wuss.

Neil   She nearly broke my fingers.

Agnes   She's always hated needles.

Neil   Has she?

Agnes   Oh yeah. I used to sit on her legs when we went for blood tests.

Neil   That does not surprise me.

Agnes   What's that supposed to mean?

Neil   Nothing! Honestly.

. . .

She was brave today.

Agnes   She is. She's heroic, my daughter.

. . .

Neil   It was good having you there. It was important to her.

Agnes   Just because I disapprove doesn't mean she's going to have to do everything alone.

Neil   Does she know that?

Agnes   Yes. Of course. Of course she does.

. . .

You don't like that, do you?

She takes his vodka off of him, and begins drinking it herself.

Neil So you should know. Kelly and I have been talking.

Agnes Right.

Neil And if. If the results come back. And they're positive.

Agnes She wants to keep the baby.

Neil And I agree. We've talked about it. A lot. Considered every option carefully.

Agnes Right.

Neil So you need to be on board with that.

. . .

Put your feelings aside. Support.

Agnes I've been at every appointment. Every meeting.

Neil But you'll be a grandma. Not just Kelly's mum.

. . .

So. Even if the results are positive /

Agnes / Okay.

Neil Because whatever happens this baby is a gift.

Agnes Oh Christ. A gift?

Neil You don't even know you're doing it, do you?

Agnes Doing what?

Neil Kelly hears everything. Every little comment. The 'Oh Christs'.

Agnes Don't be sensitive.

Neil It really hurts her feelings.

Agnes   But it's not a gift. You shouldn't say that.

Neil   Agnes.

Agnes   No. I'd hear that all the time. When she was a kid. I'd get people, other mums mostly, telling me like they felt it was their duty, that she was a gift. A blessing. But I hated it. Stuff like that, it ignores that kids with Down's Syndrome are people. People with with their own problems.

Neil   But.

Agnes   Neil. Grow up a bit.

Neil   If you're going to be there. I won't have. She's going to need you on her side.

Agnes   I've always been on her side, Neil.

Neil   Even if you think you know better.

Agnes   Okay.

Neil   This should be a fresh start.

Agnes   I heard you the first time.

Neil   Okay. Thank you.

. . .

Agnes   And you're gonna be there?

Neil   Be there?

Agnes   Yeah. Even if everything goes tits up between you two.

Neil   We're back on track.

Agnes   And if she'd sacked you off?

Neil   I'm going to be part of the baby's life.

Agnes   You're sure about that?

Neil   Yes. Agnes.

Agnes   Because this will be the hardest thing you've ever done.

Neil   I love your daughter. We can make this work.

Agnes   You think you would cope with a kid with Down's Syndrome as well as Kelly?

Neil   Kelly's Down's Syndrome is the least interesting thing about her.

Agnes   But you can't just ignore it.

Neil   I didn't. The first time Kelly went to hold my hand. My instinct was to let go. I caught myself thinking, for a split second, that I should stop.

Agnes   But you didn't.

Neil   No. But worrying about what other people might think meant we kissed much later than I wanted to. I'm not an idiot, Agnes. I know what people say. See how they treat us. But that's their problem. Kelly has every right to be loved. By anyone she chooses. No one else should give a fuck.

Agnes   It's not the same as loving anyone else.

Neil   Of course it is.

Agnes   No it isn't. You have to look after her. Love her with your wits about ya. Protect her.

Neil   You can't wrap her up in cotton wool.

Agnes   Can't I?

Neil   She has to go out into the world. Try stuff. Fuck up.

Agnes   Like it or not, Neil, she's vulnerable. And there are people out there who are dumb. And won't understand her and won't try to.

Neil   But they're rare.

Agnes   No. They're not.

Neil   Not everyone is out to get her.

Agnes   Do you know what happened with the morning-after pill?

. . .

Neil   It didn't work.

Agnes   She never got it.

. . .

Neil · But.

Agnes   I finally got the truth out of her a few weeks ago. She took the money you gave her and went into Harris's. Just like she said she would. But she couldn't find the pharmacy bit. It's confusing for her, so she does what I've taught her to do and asks someone for help. Someone in uniform. Who she can trust. Get them to point her in the right direction. So she walks up to this sales girl and asks her if she can take her to the pharmacist. The girl asks why, what does she need? Maybe she thinks Kelly is confused. I dunno. Kelly isn't shy so she tells her that she needs the morning-after pill. Hell, knowing Kelly, she probably loved shocking her. And do you know what the girl does? She laughs in her face.

. . .

Neil   Jesus. I didn't –

Agnes   She's laughed at. The girl tells her not to be daft. Assumes she's. She looks at her and all she can see is Down's Syndrome.

Neil   Agnes.

Agnes   No, she does, Neil. Because like it or not, when most people really have to look at it. Stare it in the face. They can't see past it and they're cruel. And that's what I have to protect her from and you didn't do that. Because she was made to feel this big. And now.

Neil   She told me she did. I dropped her off before work. I wanted to wait with her because. But. She tod me she didn't need her boyfriend standing over her and if I didn't trust her to do it then /

Agnes   I don't care what she told you, she was ashamed. You should've been with her.

Neil   She wanted to do it on her own. If I'd known any of this . . .

Agnes   Neil. There are some things you have to do with her. Because most of the time caring for Kelly literally means caring for her.

Neil   I'm sorry.

Agnes   Not everyone will be out to get you but you've got to assume they are. It's the only way to survive.

Neil   I know that I should have been with her. But. Still. Kelly deserves to do more than survive.

Agnes   Don't you think I'd like to be different with her?

. . .

I have to know she's going to be okay.

Neil   She will be.

Agnes   Well I won't be around for ever. So. Enjoy being the fun one whilst it lasts.

Neil   You do know she thinks the world of you, don't you?

. . .

She pours herself another vodka.

For the record, I don't blame you.

Agnes   For what?

Neil   Wanting her to be with someone else.

Agnes   Ha! Regardless of Down's Syndrome, I was never going to like her boyfriend.

Neil   Thanks.

Agnes   I just didn't want to have to stand and watch while her heart broke.

. . .

You're very kind to her.

Neil   I try.

Agnes   Although I still don't know what she sees in you.

She smiles.

Thank you. For coming over.

Neil   And thank you for the vodka.

Agnes   Lightweight.

May

Neil *and* **Kelly** *on the beach. She's finally got him there. She is rubbing sun cream into his back.*

Kelly   Maybe it's too complicated for them.

Neil   There's a *huge* difference between the two.

Kelly   Really?

Neil   Please.

Kelly   Oh God. Go on then.

Neil   People like Spiderman or Captain America are converts, they get their powers through science or outside interventions. They're mutates. They transform. He's literally bitten by a spider and that turns him into Spiderman, but before that he's just a regular human. He's Peter Parker. If it weren't for that spider, he'd be bog-standard like the rest of us. But mutants like Wolverine, all the X-men. They're special, different from birth. It's prenatal and they usually develop their powers during puberty when their bodies start to change anyway. But they get these powers because of their genetic make-up. *The X-gene.* People understand Spiderman because they can explain him, and because he is still essentially Peter Parker. But mutants. They don't have an alter ego. They are committed. They aren't like superheroes who can blend in, so people fear them. And hunt them. That's the fundamental difference. And if you don't get that, then you shouldn't even be on the message boards in the first place. Honestly, people online call themselves fans but they're actually so uninformed.

Kelly Are you finished?

Neil Was I boring you?

Kelly No! I'm teasing. You seem stressed.

Neil I am.

Kelly Really?

Neil Yeah! I'm fucking terrified. About all of this.

She looks at him.

Neil I know I'm meant to. But. Soon there will be a baby. A real baby that will need stuff from us and it will be our job to make sure they're safe and not a murderer and have manners. It's. A lot.

. . .

Kelly I wanna give you something. Grab my bag.

Neil It's just there.

She gestures to her pregnant belly.

He wipes his hands on the towel. He passes her the bag. She gets out a small box and hands it to him. He opens it. It's a piece of amber.

What is it?

Kelly   Amber. It's rare. And special.

Neil   It's beautiful.

Kelly   Will you marry me?

He smiles. She's serious.

Neil   Yeah.

Kelly   Good.

Neil   I love you.

She lies down.

Kelly   Great. Because I'm not having this baby be called a bastard.

June

The beach. Early morning. **Agnes** *is sat on her coat and* **Kelly** *is wandering around. A huge jellyfish has been washed up on to shore.*

Agnes   Taxi'll be five minutes.

Kelly   I should be there.

Agnes   You needed a rest. Neil's fine on his own.

. . .

It's a big one ain't it? Biggest one I've ever seen. And it don't look like the gulls have got to it much either.

Kelly   I like jellyfish.

Agnes   They're horrible.

Kelly   I think they're cool.

Agnes   Why don't you sit down?

Kelly   Can't.

Agnes   I thought it might relax you a bit, coming here.

Kelly   The last place in the universe I wanna be is here.

Agnes   Kelly.

Kelly   I wanna know what she feels like.

Agnes   You'll get to hold her soon.

Kelly   You don't know that. You're just saying that.

Agnes   I'm not. I'm just trying to /

Kelly   / What?

Agnes   I dunno.

Kelly   You're just making noise.

Agnes   Don't get yourself worked up again. This is why we thought it would be good for you to get away from the hospital for a bit. Fresh air.

Kelly   I'm sick and tired of people knowing what's good for me.

Agnes   Everyone is doing their best, Kel. Neil's worried about you.

Kelly   Nobody should be worried about me. What about her? She's like china. She could break.

. . .

Do you think it's my fault? Mum?

Agnes   We knew after the test that she'd have Down's Syndrome.

Kelly   But I did it anyway.

Agnes   Kelly. You do know that she's beautiful – don't you?

. . .

Kelly   Do you wish I'd gotten rid of her?

Agnes   What a question.

Kelly Do you?

Agnes No, love. I don't. Don't torture yourself. She came early. Babies do that sometimes.

Kelly She can't breathe.

Agnes They're just being cautious. You heard what he said.

. . .

You know when you were born. The midwife was more surprised than I was. Because I was so young.

Kelly Right.

Agnes You came early. Like her. The midwife didn't even have time to put her gloves on.

Kelly Gross.

Agnes And then they whisked you off, and they didn't bring you back – not for hours. And when the doctor did eventually turn up the first thing she said to me was. First, I want to tell that your daughter is adorable.

Kelly *smiles*.

Agnes And I still hadn't seen you. I just wanted to know what you looked like. And then she was saying something about your features being consistent with. And I'm thinking. What the fuck is this woman talking about?

Kelly Mum.

Agnes And when she said Down's Syndrome. I did cry. I was sad about it. And my mum had no idea what to do because she was. She thought she deserved more from life. But no one had died. So I told myself even if it killed me, I'd be smiling the first time I held you. And I made good on that promise. Big dopey grin. And I never liked smiling 'cos I've got goat's teeth.

Kelly Did you think I was ugly?

Agnes   No. No.

Kelly   What if you'd known? Before.

Agnes   I didn't.

Kelly   But . . .

Agnes   I didn't. And I wouldn't change ya.

Kelly   I just know how hard it's going to be for her.

. . .

Kelly   Can I have a hug please?

Agnes   Course, course you can.

They hug one another really tightly.

Kelly *goes to pull away first.*

Agnes   No. You're not ready yet.

They hug some more.

Kelly *pulls away.*

Kelly   I have a headache.

Agnes   You should drink something.

Kelly   I'm not thirsty.

Agnes   But if you drink something it might make your headache go away. Sometimes that works.

Kelly   Today I wanna take a photo of her.

Agnes   That's fine, we can do that.

Kelly   Just in case.

Agnes   No, Kelly.

Kelly   I was looking forward to bringing her here.

Agnes   You can still look forward to things like that. The doctors said that under the circumstances she's doing really well.

Kelly   I thought we could show her where to find starfish.

Agnes   That will be nice. I'd like that.

Kelly   And when you die, me and her would still do the walk together. We'd carry it on. I was looking forward to that.

Agnes   Thanks.

Kelly   I'm going to look at the jellyfish.

Agnes   Well don't get mucky.

Kelly   Mum.

Agnes   Sorry.

Kelly   Come with me?

They both go and look at the jellyfish.

Agnes   The sea will be back in to take it away again soon.

Kelly   Look. You can see right through it.

Agnes   I guess that's the idea. If you can't be seen, I imagine it'd be easier to catch things to eat.

Kelly   I wonder what it's like. If you don't have a face. If they just look right through. Like you're nothing. That's terrible.

. . .

Agnes   Big, ain't it?

Kelly   Poor thing.

Agnes   It reeks.

Kelly   Well it is dead.

Agnes   It's disgusting.

She goes and picks up a bit of wood that's been washed up by the sea.

Kelly What are you doing?

Agnes I can't look at it no more.

She begins moving down the beach like it's toxic waste.

Kelly Leave it alone. It can still sting you.

Agnes No it can't.

Kelly Yes it can.

Agnes Gross.

Kelly Stop it.

Agnes I'm just moving it.

Kelly *turns and walks away.*

Agnes What? Where're you going?

Kelly Don't come running to me when it does sting you.

Agnes Wait up.

*She drops the piece of wood and goes after **Kelly**.*

Agnes Warmer than it was last year ain't it? It gets warmer so much earlier now.

Kelly You always say that.

Agnes No I don't.

Kelly You do. Every year.

Agnes's *phone goes off.*

Kelly Who is it?

Agnes Taxi. He'll be five minutes.

Kelly He said that five minutes ago.

Agnes Well I'm sure he's doing his best.

Kelly   Then why lie?

Agnes   Why would anyone, Kelly, try and upset you and make your life more difficult? Why would I do that? Why would anyone do that?

Kelly   Don't shout at me.

Agnes   I'm not shouting at you.

Kelly   You can shout without raising your voice.

Agnes   Okay. I'm sorry. Okay.

Kelly   My headache is really bad now.

Agnes   I've got some paracetamol in my bag; you can take that.

Kelly   Have you got a yoghurt?

Agnes   No.

Kelly   I can't take them unless they're in a yoghurt.

Agnes   Well I've not got one.

Kelly   I can't swallow them. They're disgusting.

Agnes   Well you're gonna have to try.

Kelly   I can't.

Agnes   You've just given birth. Don't tell me you can't handle a paracetamol.

Kelly   This is so hard.

Agnes   I know, sweetheart.

Kelly   Please make it better. Sort it out for me.

Agnes   I wish I could.

Kelly   What if I can't do this?

Agnes Look at everything else that you've done. I am so proud of you. And I know she's gonna surprise ya, prove ya wrong, every chance she gets. Trust me. She will.

. . .

Kelly Thank you. For bringing me here.

Agnes That's okay.

Kelly I'm going to have to change my shoes. I can't take sand into the hospital.

Agnes That's a good idea.

. . .

Look. I'm sorry that I wasn't sure whether you'd be able to do this. In the beginning.

Kelly But you're my mum.

Agnes I know and I let you down. I was worried about you.

Kelly Because I'm disabled?

Agnes Yes. I know that's wrong. But yes.

. . .

Kelly What about people who can't make friends? Or who don't laugh and are full of no love? They're the real disabilities. I think.

Agnes *takes* **Kelly**'s *hand in hers.*

Kelly Mum?

Agnes Yeah?

Kelly She's going to be okay, yeah?

Agnes Yeah. I told ya.

Kelly I'm calling her Daisy.

Agnes Right. Bit wet, ain't it?

Kelly   Names are important.

Agnes   I'll get used to it.

. . .

Kelly   I'm going to take such good care of her.

She looks out at the sea.

Just watch me.

Methuen Drama Modern Plays

include work by

Bola Agbaje
Edward Albee
Davey Anderson
Jean Anouilh
John Arden
Peter Barnes
Sebastian Barry
Alistair Beaton
Brendan Behan
Edward Bond
William Boyd
Bertolt Brecht
Howard Brenton
Amelia Bullmore
Anthony Burgess
Leo Butler
Jim Cartwright
Lolita Chakrabarti
Caryl Churchill
Lucinda Coxon
Curious Directive
Nick Darke
Shelagh Delaney
Ishy Din
Claire Dowie
David Edgar
David Eldridge
Dario Fo
Michael Frayn
John Godber
Paul Godfrey
James Graham
David Greig
John Guare
Mark Haddon
Peter Handke
David Harrower
Jonathan Harvey
Iain Heggie

Robert Holman
Caroline Horton
Terry Johnson
Sarah Kane
Barrie Keeffe
Doug Lucie
Anders Lustgarten
David Mamet
Patrick Marber
Martin McDonagh
Arthur Miller
D. C. Moore
Tom Murphy
Phyllis Nagy
Anthony Neilson
Peter Nichols
Joe Orton
Joe Penhall
Luigi Pirandello
Stephen Poliakoff
Lucy Prebble
Peter Quilter
Mark Ravenhill
Philip Ridley
Willy Russell
Jean-Paul Sartre
Sam Shepard
Martin Sherman
Wole Soyinka
Simon Stephens
Peter Straughan
Kate Tempest
Theatre Workshop
Judy Upton
Timberlake Wertenbaker
Roy Williams
Snoo Wilson
Frances Ya-Chu Cowhig
Benjamin Zephaniah

For a complete listing of
Methuen Drama titles, visit:
www.bloomsbury.com/drama

Follow us on Twitter and keep up to date
with our news and publications
@MethuenDrama